WILEY BUCK AND OTHER STORIES
OF THE CONCORD COMMUNITY

Wiley Buck and Other Stories of the Concord Community

By

HENRY McGILBERT WAGSTAFF

With an Editorial Note
by
LOUIS R. WILSON

Chapel Hill
THE UNIVERSITY OF NORTH CAROLINA PRESS

Copyright, 1953, by
THE UNIVERSITY OF NORTH CAROLINA PRESS

Editorial Note

The stories and sketches embraced in *Wiley Buck and Other Stories of the Concord Community* fall into the category of social history. They deal with the Concord community, a well-defined, influential pre- and post-Civil War neighborhood in Person County, North Carolina, during the period 1850-1900.

As genre pictures they bring into sharp focus the daily life of the people at home, at church, in the store, in the field, and in all the activities that engaged a farming community in the post-Civil War era.

In particular, they reveal the limitless interests of an inquisitive, imaginative boy as he visited his traps, fished and swam in the near-by streams, attended the annual revivals, camped overnight with the wagons carrying tobacco to the nearest market, attended the neighborhood school, visited the Negro cabins—interests that made up his boyhood world and gave it infinite variety and charm.

They also perform another service. They preserve in vivid form events and customs and characters of a bygone day. In them much of the past now gone is caught in clear focus. The "Captains" of the post-war era, incapable of adjustment to new conditions, are seen as they passed off the stage. The revivalist, whipping up the emotion of his congregation to the shouting pitch, is fixed in sharp perspective. The plodding plow horse and the family carriage are recalled to mind now that they have given place to tractor and automobile. Likewise, the tobacco barn formerly fired with oak and hickory from the adjoining woods but now with oil are clearly reproduced. And the Negro boy companions, the Negro "Uncles" and "Aunts" of the Cabin who gave endless variety and interest to a small boy's world are pictured in their setting in a generation that is past.

The author, Henry McGilbert Wagstaff, Professor of History in the University of North Carolina, 1907-45, was a member of the Concord community. He was born within it on January 27, 1875, and his wife was a member of an adjoining community. He retained a part of his father's estate and during his connection with the University as Professor of History, he carried on farming operations through tenants and maintained close connection with members of his family who continued to live within the community. In summer, when tobacco was growing or ripening, he would frequently look at the clouds gathering forty miles away where his fields lay, and wonder whether they were in the path of the fructifying rain.

The stories and sketches were written in the late 1930's and early 1940's. One, "The Revival," was read before the North Carolina State Literary and Historical Association in December, 1944, and published in *The North Carolina Historical Review* in January, 1946. All evidence the abiding interest of the author in the life with which he was familiar in his boyhood, and which he has depicted with artistry and skill.

LOUIS R. WILSON

Chapel Hill, N. C.
November 1, 1952

Contents

Editorial Note
PAGE V

The Concord Community in Retrospect
PAGE 3

Memories
PAGE 19

Our Two Captains
PAGE 38

The Revival
PAGE 57

Uncle Calvin and His Five Sons
PAGE 73

Abimelech Matthew Jordan, Colporteur
PAGE 88

The Quick-Witted Young Man
PAGE 101

Wiley Buck
PAGE 104

"Old Man" John Bradsher—a Ghost Story
PAGE 116

WILEY BUCK AND OTHER STORIES
OF THE CONCORD COMMUNITY

The Concord Community
In Retrospect

The Concord community, in North Carolina's Person County, should perhaps first be defined in terms of its church, Concord, since the church, in popular speech, gives name to the community. This church is Methodist and its name has a pleasing connotation of peace and harmony. The name and its implications, however, have not always been taken too literally by the group of people who worship here. Its members have been rather notably individualistic, and teamwork has not always been esteemed a virtue. Geographically the community was at an earlier date a sprawling, irregular area with less compactness than now characterizes it. Then it was as if its parts were caught up between other forming communities, or gathered in from left-overs. The church itself was in a handsome grove of oak trees, then in their prime. This grove stood at the juncture of a comparatively young road which at this point was flung off eastward from the old road that was the real axis of the Concord section sixty and seventy years ago. This old road journeyed out of Leasburg on the western county line, tended eastward by Thaxton's Gate and on across the hills of the South Hyco and the Little Duck and, at Concord, turned again in a generally northern direction toward the Hycotee and Virginia. This road, as if it belonged to the hills, seemed loath to enter the heavily timbered and less broken country lying eastward from Concord toward the county seat. This latter area was then known as "The Big Woods," and consisted of heavy timber of original oaks interspersed with huge straight pines, the then aristocrats of the forest. These woods covered mellow, loamy, gray soil, good for tobacco culture, and so were destined to pass away as this crop spread out of the coarser soil of the hills north and west. In my own memory is the sight of whole blocks of beautiful timber, cut down, rolled together, and fired, for the land upon which it recently stood. Now that same area has its few clumps of young pines, and the majesty of real trees seldom meets the eye. But it is far from the purpose of this little retrospect to point out either economic or social errors of my community. These things are products of wide-sweeping forces which few communities, little or big, rarely generate the wisdom to evade in advance of experience.

I have noted that the axis of our community was the old road from Leasburg to Concord. This should, of course, be restricted to the eastern half—from Thaxton's Gate to Concord. West of Thaxton's Gate the people generally belonged to the Leasburg community and worshipped there; east, they belonged to Concord. At the Gate an old road from Milton way joined our road after passing across the North Hyco and Cobb Creek hills and lastly through the Thaxton property. From the Gate to Concord Church was about six miles, with Olive Hill, the country store and post office about half way. Olive Hill was on the ridge between the South Hyco and its tributary, the Little Duck, at the point where a ridge road from the south came down to join the main road. This place came nearer being the geographical center of the community at that time than did Concord Church, which was on its eastern edge.

Leasburg to the west, Lea's Chapel to the southwest, and Oak Grove to the northeast were the distinctive Methodist Church communities adjacent, while overlapping elements of other denominations spread in other directions. There were the Ebenezer and Sunny Side communities, the first between Leasburg and Lea's Chapel; the second blocking in Lea's Chapel on the east. Both these were Primitive Baptist; toward the north one felt that our community shaded off into Missionary Baptist affiliation with Ephesus as its center. These boundaries, here so indefinitely fixed, actually existed only in the habits of thinking and acting of the people; yet community self-consciousness was

The Concord Community in Retrospect 5

fairly strong. You *belonged* to your community. The young people, particularly, passed from one of these church communities to another as a Sunday adventure and formed attachments far and near. Even the elders, now and then in groups, did the same thing, visiting the church of some neighboring community on preaching day and taking dinner in the home of friends near by. This practice was facilitated by the fact that the Methodist churches mentioned usually constituted a "circuit" of a minister, each church having its fixed Sunday in the month for preaching services. Hence it naturally became the habit to speak of Sundays as "first Sunday," "second Sunday," etc., and one was a man grown before he thought of Sundays by an actual date in the calendar. Three Sundays in the month, only Sunday School at one's local church offered opportunity for recreation and contacts. Therefore the active and spirited young were apt to forge further afield and attend the church where preaching was due on that particular Sunday and where a larger crowd consequently gathered.

The people who made up the Concord community, then as now, were almost uniformly of English stock, as attested by their names. There were Thaxtons (one main family), Winsteads (most numerous), Wagstaffs (next most numerous), Sergeants, Paylors, Days, Bradshers, Williamses, Featherstones, Woods, Clays, Brookses, and others who stand out less clearly in my memory. Sixty years ago the elders of these families were the generation that had come through the strain and wreckage of the Civil War. Nearly all the men had served as soldiers in that conflict and, their cause defeated, they had witnessed the passing of the economic and social order their youth had known. Theirs was the task of rebuilding a livable way of life. Traditional ways and habits were no longer possible. Land they had in abundance, but labor forms were still in transition and unsettlement. Land-ownership offered some security but little prosperity. Some had never worked the soil with their own hands and found it difficult to learn this necessity. Some refused to try, and acquiesced in an ever-declining standard of living. Some were of sterner stuff and maintained morale by sturdy struggle. Some sought supplementary income in activities apart from land cultivation or its management. But the keeping of a country store by a man untrained in merchandizing arts had its defects in a rural community without money or a reviving agriculture. A country medical or dental practice in such a community had its great handicaps, beside the meagre opportunity for training in these or any of the professions. But there were representatives in our community of these several endeavors and they are a part of the picture I should like to bring into focus of the people of that generation. Not a few of this generation lived past the turn of the century and are thus not so difficult to pass in review.

Doctor Joe Thaxton was quite an elderly man at my earliest memory. In fact, I think of him as the "senior" in the Concord community. Yet he was an active man, possessing great vigor of mind and body. His home was some half-mile from the Gate, up a very straight road which ran through heavy timber the whole way except for one indentation near the house where a splendid orchard of fruit trees—apple, peach, and cherry— was cultivated. His house was large and of good architecture, well placed amidst a heavy grove of handsome trees among which stood also numerous other well-built service structures. Perhaps Dr. Thaxton's place in the hill country between the two Hycos was the most nearly typical southern slave plantation in our area. The Doctor had owned something over a hundred slaves until the end of the Civil War, and had kept up all the attractive forms of country life the pre-war era made possible. And yet I doubt that his large landed estate was truly prosperous, even though its owner possessed great energy and had some scientific ideas on agriculture. I suspect the lure of supplemental income was why he had taken to medical practice when a young man. And yet his practice was no mere side-activity. He took the profession seriously, respected it, had had good training somewhere, went night or day where his services were required, and was held to be a most excellent physician. He was a widower, but his three daughters, one beautiful, and two notably handsome, made his home a place of liveliness, though always with dignity and culture. There were two sons also, both musical, both social-minded. The eldest went away early and I remember little of him except that he was a polished and attractive man. The younger son, named for his father, tried futilely, after his father's death, to carry on the plantation; but he was more at home on the back of a fast black mare, named Polky, than in the uncongenial task of inducing Negro "croppers" to get up early in the morning. Yet he gave me a kid billy-goat, and I have pleasant memories of him.

Grandy Winstead, the finest-grained of a large family of brothers, for years kept a store at Olive Hill, an old trade center that had seen better days in pre-war times. He owned a large and hilly farm through which ran both the South Hyco and the Little Duck before they met below. His home crowned the highest knoll on the ridge between these streams. The site of his home was well chosen. The architecture of his house (not large) was simple and graceful. Its grounds were spacious, with good trees, and heavily planted to large English boxwood in walks and circles. Below the house, at the juncture of roads, stood his store, an oblong structure with a full-length porch in front under the continuing roof. At one end was an annex, with a double chimney, which served the store as well. This annex "Uncle Grandy" generously placed at the disposal of the community for its three or four months public school.

Across from the store in an angle formed by the roads was the chief community blacksmith shop, where people brought horses and mules to be shod and wheels to be re-tired. The smith was a Negro named Daniel Howertown, and all the children, at "big" and "little" recess, found its activities a source of perennial interest. "Uncle" Jerry Medley, a Negro, was the mail carrier. He brought one mail a day, on horseback, the mail in a locked leather pouch, fitted to balance on either side when placed under the rider's seat. Uncle Grandy kept the key to the pouch. Often, not too busy in the store, he sat in contemplative mood on the porch and watched across the long hill beyond the Little Duck for Uncle Jerry to come in sight. Sometimes he would remark, "Well, yon comes Jerry," or, "Well, Jerry is late today." Uncle Grandy possessed a serene and gentle spirit, though quite befogged by the changing order of his time. He found much comfort in religion and its services.

He conducted the Sunday School at Concord Church for many years and gave it the atmosphere of religious worship. His wife, "Miss Bettie" (to all younger generations), was a gracious lady who preserved to her death the manners and customs of an earlier day.

I learned at least one profitable lesson at school here at the old store, though some might call it clever graft. At "big" recess I would listen for the cackle of hens at the granary and barn, down the slope from the house on the hill. If these cackles had a certain joyous and exultant sound I would slip away from play, mosey about in the barn, gather up the fresh-laid egg, or eggs, and take them up the hill to Miss Bettie. My reward was uniformly a little square of golden pound-cake, a delicacy for which I have always had a very keen tooth. My own mother's cakes at home, of this my favorite kind, were never excelled anywhere, by anybody; but the distance between them there seemed much too long. Hence these gleanings from the hands of Miss Bettie for gathering up her eggs seemed all to the good. Besides, those eggs were laid by the foolish hens in the horse-troughs and so would have been promptly destroyed but for my foresight, a foresight sharpened by the lure of pound-cake.

Of a number of brothers of Uncle Grandy Winstead two stood out sufficiently to leave distinctive impressions. The first, Colonel C. S. Winstead, was not strictly of the Concord community. His home was in the Lea's Chapel neighborhood and he was affiliated with that church. He became a lawyer about the Civil War period, represented Person County for a time in the state legislature, and had had some appointive post under the Confederate Government. He was shrewd in business management as in his law practice and, in this double role, built up a considerable estate, mostly in land scattered widely over the northwestern section of the county. He never married and therefore left no legitimate descendants. But without doubt he left a more lasting influence upon the lives of a numerous body of younger relatives in or of the Concord community than any other man. His material success, resulting from his shrewd

The Concord Community in Retrospect

business acumen, became a sort of tradition which has not been neglected by imitators in his family connection.

Another brother of Uncle Grandy's, Uncle Jack Winstead, illustrated still different characteristics. He, the father of a large family of sons and daughters, was a Puritan fundamentalist and emphasized in his life the stern doctrine of personal toil. He accepted literally the biblical maxim that "by the sweat of thy face shalt thou eat bread." He was a quiet and reserved man, keeping his own counsel, locking the door to all emotional outlets save one—he could be stirred to loosening his iron self-control by emotional religious appeals from the pulpit. My clearest memory-picture of him is of a rather tall old gentleman, with a long white beard, unobtrusively clapping his hands in his pew while the tears flowed down his face during the climax of a revival service. Indeed Uncle Jack's release of emotion was the climax itself. His wife, Aunt Mary, was an older sister of my father, and, though I remember her but vaguely, my picture is that of a portly, handsome, and sweet-spirited woman, given to much care about her large family.

Uncle Will Wagstaff was a stalwart of the Concord community and church. An older brother of my father, he lived near the church, and his home was a center of generous and quite slap-dash hospitality—in church season and out. This characteristic of his home was a projection of the spirit of his wife, Anna Williams, whose large brood of sons and daughters reflected their mother's philosophy, which was: "Enjoy the day." Uncle Will himself was inclined toward the principle of strict discipline, both for himself and family; but he was never quite able to accomplish results in the latter. He was a good manager of his rather large estate, strict in exacting the labor due from his help, and was known as a "good provider." His children had great and abiding respect for him, perhaps a little fear also, but it generally stopped short of imitation of his self-discipline. He was portly in appearance, wore an iron-grey beard, and walked with a strong heavy stick. I never saw him display emotion in church or out. He kept his temper in check even in circumstances where this was a rather quixotic virtue.

Uncle Ben Brooks lived near Uncle Will's, in the old house of my grandfather, Briton Wagstaff. He had married the youngest sister of my father, Aunt Belle. I remember his beard as bronzed; and that his affliction was being a Baptist, a fault for which his wife would often apologize. Yet sometimes she would smooth the shortcoming by conceding that he was a "good man" nevertheless. They could not get together on infant baptism. I have wondered if Uncle Ben's objections were founded on doctrinal conviction, or grew out of his man's aversion to too frequent marching up the aisle of the church with the newest infant in his arms to receive the few drops of Methodist-sprinkled water. There was a long string of children in that family.

Captain Robert Williams was *in* the Concord community, rather than *of* it. He was a non-conformist in matters social and religious—and didn't care. If the order in which he was reared (and liked) changed he would be damned if he would change with it. The earth owed him a living—at least his own land did —and he expected it to meet his obligation without assistance from him. He would enjoy himself, and after his own fashion. He had no impulse whatever to bend his back to the soil or his spirit to business. He was all for the joy of living. I never saw him at church and I doubt if he had any religious philosophy at all. If he had been told, as he surely would have been in church, that the Devil would get him, his probable response would have been "*bedamned* to him!" Of course Captain Robert's morale and person ran down, as did his estate; for his type of individualism is difficult to maintain without income. But he had a large love for the woods and streams. Perhaps his spirit found these the most congenial. He loved the lazy life of the fishing stretches on the Hyco, which ran through his lands, and would sit all the day on its banks for perch and knotty-head. When the timber had been cut from the hills and the low grounds were annually flooded, making them useless for cultivation, the beaver and the muskrat made a temporary return to the debris-clogged stream. Then Captain Robert, never a conservationist, took to the role of trapper and in a few years cleaned out the optimistic re-settlers.

The Concord Community in Retrospect

I have the dear memory of a truant morning from Sabbath School in which I floated along the stream with him in a crude flat-bottomed boat to visit his trap line. This great morning netted us seventeen muskrats, four beavers, and an otter. This was the peak of his season and, I think, of his whole trapping career. But it was excitement while it lasted, even to a demoralized ex-slaveowner, and I shared in it. Moreover, I was in at the skinning and he sent my mother a haunch of beaver meat for a roast. Also, his pelts had a good market and for long kept his demijohn full. In this I never shared, though I often eyed it with curiosity.

Only once did Captain Robert awaken in me a wee suspicion of insincerity. We had gone all-day fishing at Connelly's Millpond, four miles distant. He traveled in broken and battered shoes; I barefoot, as was always my custom in summertime. He carried a slight limp and his corncob pipe; I carried two long fishing poles and a pail of lunch teased from my mother with her permission to go. Arrived, we fished through the morning in a borrowed boat with indifferent success. After lunch at a near-by spring we tried again. Little luck. With the sun still "two hours high" we started homeward. Half way, or less, the Captain's limp turned into the groaning progress of a snail's pace. His corns, he swore, were murdering him. My sympathies were stirred. I walked a mile back and borrowed a mule. Then I got the Captain mounted, hoping to mount myself, behind. But the dilapidated beast refused to carry double. He even refused to take on the fishing poles. I walked, but I do not remember being particularly peeved—for the Captain's wet shirt smelt abominably of fish and bad pipe. I deserted the army when we reached my home. The Captain's place was a mile further on, across the Hyco and up a long hill. How the mule got back to its owner I do not recall. Perhaps he was turned loose at night to go alone. Still, thinking back now, that theory must be faulty. For all mules at the Perkinses were but temporary sojourners. Perkins was a notable trader in that kind of stock.

Captain Robert's son, John, was also a free and unconfined spirit and cared nothing for the humdrum routine of labor.

He, in collaboration with his uncle, Dr. John Banks Bradsher, built up, or spliced together, the last pack of fox hounds that ever cried over those hills within my memory. The two leaders of the pack were named Cleveland and Blaine, and the greater reliability on the scent was always attributed to Cleveland. If the scent was cold and Blaine essayed a yelp of encouragement nevertheless, Dr. John would chuckle and say: "It's just old Blaine—lying." This black-and-tan hound never got a word of praise. I suspect it affected his character, for I have seen a cotton-tail rabbit run over him in the field and still live to tell the tale. Yet he always managed to maintain his place between Cleveland and the rest of the pack. I came to think of him as a "secondary" leader, and I am sure he fixed in my twelve-year-old mind the place of James G. Blaine in the political life of our country. This sport of fox hunting in our area must have been a revival, and it didn't last long in its poverty setting. But I remember one glorious "ride to hounds" on the bare back of a mouse-colored mule, and I was in sight when Cleveland, leading the pack, closed in on the quarry.

Dr. John Banks Bradsher was another free soul who chose his own way. He had somewhere trained for countryside medical practice and had made a beginning in that activity. But either the going got too tough or the rewards too small, or both. His enthusiasm drained away and he ceased to practice. He remained a bachelor on his plantation, never married, but took a copper-colored mistress, named Candace, and raised several sons and daughters, one of whom, Tilda, had a flare for nursing. For many years, in her strength and skill, she performed abundant services of mercy at the bedside of both her white and her colored relatives and in the community at large. Dr. John, with the cessation of practice, ceased also his social contacts with relatives and neighbors. He never attended church and only a few Mrs. Grundys made comment now and then on his manner of life.

Two other gentlemen of our community were "Uncle John" and Captain Robert Sergeant, brothers. Uncle John was a tall spare man with a slight stoop to his shoulders, who always walked with a knobbed stick. His family's home place, to

The Concord Community in Retrospect 13

which he and a beautiful sister, "Cousin Delphia," had fallen heirs, was about one mile from Thaxton's Gate on the Leasburg Road. It was then a lovely old ante-bellum house in the midst of a grove of great elms and oaks and at the end of two rows of sycamores, between which the house road ran down to meet the main road a quarter-mile distant. Boxwood interspersed the trees on the front side.

Uncle John had married just before or during the Civil War and his wife had died early. He never ventured again and he and his maiden sister lived out their days at the old place. Cousin Delphia was younger than Uncle John and Captain Robert. Admired by the whole countryside, she particularly inspired the romantic fervor of Dr. John Banks Bradsher, before his social dénouement. He attended her parties in a high beaver hat and the other elegant accouterments of the correct gentleman. I have heard my mother tell with great amusement of seeing Cousin Delphia trip down the stairway, with a bevy of girl friends about her, to the hall where gentlemen's hats were hung and, before entering the parlor to greet her admirers, select the Doctor's beaver, set it on the floor and place her foot in it—thus to show in what regard she held the suit of this particular gentleman.

Uncle John's frame was never built for a wrestle with the soil, and was never apprenticed to it. He walked around in a slow and hazy way to view the "croppers" at work; but he much preferred to tramp off and visit with neighbors—the Thaxtons, the Paylors, or my father's house, these three being the nearest by. He was a gentle soul, bore no malice to any man, and showed great courtesy to old and young in a sort of ponderous way. The circumstances of his death and "shrouding" are deep burnt into my memory. This last rite was, at the command of my father, performed by a tenant farmer and myself—I, who was fourteen years old and always afraid of ghosts. I had great respect, even liking, for Uncle John; but I trembled for years at the recollection of that ordeal.

Captain Robert Sergeant, Uncle John's brother, slightly younger, was a man of a different cast, both in look and outlook. He was slighter of frame, erect, alert, and livelier in movement. His land was a division of the old Sergeant home place cut off on the southeast side. On it was a good owner's house and tenant houses round about. But Captain Robert, like Captain Robert Williams, was not an agriculturist, and never aspired to be. Whether his captaincy was acquired in the Civil War, or whether it was "courtesy," I do not remember; I believe the former. I know he had been a soldier.

Captain Robert elected to merchandise, and set up a store at the junction of roads just by Concord Church. He was there when the district school was for a time moved from Olive Hill to Concord, and there, as a child, I had a chance to compare Captain Robert's with Uncle Grandy's generosity at the ginger cake barrel. Uncle Grandy, at Olive Hill, had sometimes given you one—if you hadn't your penny. Captain Robert always waited on the show of your coin. To me this was quite sufficient grounds to move the school back to its former place. Those were unrivaled cakes, as big as a saucer, and with such gingery flavor! And yet I do not now believe Captain Robert was a "stingy" man. Perhaps he felt it was good soldierly discipline. Or perhaps because he had no children of his own he had not learned childhood's point of view. He never married, but was quite social-minded. He loved music and was proficient with the violin and the accordion, the latter an instrument quite popular in that period. He, too, loved to visit the homes of his friends, bringing his instruments along to the great pleasure of the grown-ups. Also he liked to serenade Miss Willie Lea, of Leasburg, a cultured maiden lady who stimulated his intellect, called out his courtly manners, and at the same time titillated his heart. This romance never matured. The story ran that Miss Willie took caution to her counsel in face of Captain Robert's ever-growing addiction to his cups. And yet 'twas in his cups that his manners were at perfection.

I do not recall Captain Robert as having any church connection, though Uncle John and Cousin Delphia were good Methodists. The church then divided drinkers from non-drinkers. A church member, if he indulged, "fell from grace" thereby, and to regain that state must needs make public pro-

The Concord Community in Retrospect 15

testation of repentance and a re-affirmation of purpose to follow the straight and narrow way. Captains Robert Sergeant and Robert Williams, mavericks both, would have pronounced such proceedings as falderal and gone about their—well, their relaxations.

Uncles Jim and Henry Paylor were my blood uncles on my mother's side. Uncle Jim's place was adjoining ours and about a mile from Thaxton's Gate. The home had a good site on a gentle crest sloping down to the road just south. Across the road was a wooded lot of fine oaks and hickories, among which stood tobacco barns. This place I knew in its every foot, as I did our own, and all its inhabitants, white and black. Uncle Jim was a small-framed man, with a spade beard. Neither he nor Uncle Henry had talent for farming, but Uncle Jim tried it in a stubborn sort of way. Indeed he was a stubborn man all through. And yet his was not the strongest personality in his household. This was Aunt Anne, who had been a Walker and whom Uncle Jim had married on Castle Creek in the Woodsdale neighborhood. She was a positive character and determined to let no circumstance balk the process of getting along. To her many other virtues she added a passion for work, neatness, and cleanliness. It was generally held that her sons' wives and her married nieces swept and garnished their whole houses, even under the beds, when expecting a visit from Aunt Anne. She was reported to kneel down for her prayers and place the palm of her hand on floors under beds to see if dirt and dust were there. She loved to set out good food, and none was ever better than hers. Her mutton, her sausage with sage, her perfect butter, with hot, light, flaky biscuits, her preserves of peach, quince, and cherry, her honey, her cool sweet milk; and the hospitality with which she urged all these upon you until you could hold no more—what a deep furrow they made in my memory!

Aunt Anne also raised her family—three sons and a sweet and gentle daughter—in the fear and admonition of the Lord. It was her duty, and she did not neglect it. Well I remember her parting thrust to her youngest son, "Little Jimmy," and to me—a Little Jimmy follower—as we started off to the swimming hole on Saturday afternoon after wringing her reluctant consent: "Well if you go and get drowned and come back here I shall whip you both to a frazzle!" And so I made up my mind then and there not to come back if I was drowned.

But Uncle Jim, I felt, was more of a problem to Aunt Anne than her sons and daughter and her small nephew, who was so often about. They were biddable; but not he. As I have said, he was a stubborn man, though not of that type of stubbornness that shows up in a loud clash of words. He was silently stubborn, that type my sister characterized as "Paylor mule." Aunt Anne's arrows of suggestion and direction glanced off him as if he had not heard. He loved to read and I had a notion that Aunt Anne held his reading to be a ruse, at very best a waste of time. But this did not disturb Uncle Jim. He read on, only now and again fumbling for his ornamental snuff-box from which, after tapping the lid with his finger, he would take a pinch to his nose and deliver himself of a hearty sneeze. He was the only man I remember of that generation who clung to the snuffing habit, brought over from pre-war days. And I have wondered if that was stubbornness too.

Uncle Henry was of another physical and mental pattern. He was larger and carried more flesh. He too wore a beard, white and rather thin, and walked with a cane, as many of his contemporaries did. As he grew old he walked about from place to place somewhat restlessly. The best story I recall of him was about his presence at an illicit "still" one afternoon when revenue officers raided the hidden place. All ran, and so escaped, except Uncle Henry. He of all the company stood his ground; but he apologized to the officers of the law in not showing them the respect of flight. His reason: he "had heart trouble, and so couldn't run." The officers respected his role of visitor and acted on the wise assumption that only the guilty flee. Uncle Henry was a regular churchman, but I think he preferred the after-service sessions out under the trees in converse with his friends.

Dr. Bill Bradsher, a landowner on the ridge road south from Olive Hill, was a country dentist, the only one in or near the Concord community. No churchman, he was a stay-at-home body. He cared not a whit that his office in a corner of his yard had no waiting list for his professional services. In fact he rejoiced in the health of teeth rather than in their ailments. He possessed wit and humor and knew something of the classics. He quoted poetry, sometimes from the Romans, Horace and Virgil, sometimes from the English lyricists, Keats and Shelley. He was also a lover of Byron. His version of Byron's first verse, written in Nottingham at the age of five, lingers in my memory still. The child, lame from his birth, had been cross and fretful. His superstitious old nurse had taken him out on the lawn and "plunked" (Dr. Bill's very word) him down on the grass under the shade of a tree. In his "scribble-book" (again the Doctor's word) the sprite now wrote:

> There was an old woman
> In Nottingham dwelled,
> As cross an old wench
> As ever was in Hell,
> And when she dies,
> Which I hope is soon,
> She fully believes
> She'll go to the Moon.

Dr. Bill relished this little bit of precocious poetry and always repeated it twice. It was my introduction to Byron, a stormy petrel of liberalism and revolt. I have never checked on the Doctor's version of his "first" verse; but I became nevertheless a life-long lover of Byron.

Dr. Bill was thin and lanky and alert. He liked to sit in the shade of his trees, with a glass at his hand. He was fond of cider, which he made in seasons of fruit. He made wine from his grapes; but now and again he preferred a nip of something with greater energy. His wife, "Miss Maidie," was a beautiful white-haired lady who was patient with everybody's faults and foibles; and she held a good proper cup of coffee to be the one panacea for most of the ills of life. Dr. Bill liked coffee also, though he held for another panacea.

There were other men and women of that era in this community who stand out in my early memory as possessing interesting characteristics, and I should like to project them. There were Patrick Clay, Charles Wood (father of the late Charles Turbeville Wood), John and George Wagstaff, and Bill Day. And especially my own father. The latter I am sure I should draw in colors too generous for general endorsement—a natural human frailty, I suppose, where one's very own is concerned.

Memories

My childhood home stood on a slope of the gradually descending hills that come down from the west to the Hyco River. The river bottoms below were wide, and their loamy soil was planted to corn, year in and year out. Their fertility was renewed as constantly by "freshets," which we constantly trusted would not occur in the season of crops. Often they did, but in case the seasons got mixed—as they sometimes did—and the "freshet," or flood, occurred in the period of the crop of corn, then there was great loss to the farmers whose lands included the river bottoms. This ours did, my father's acres crossing the river, and a fourth of our domain was on the east side. Many of my childhood memories are linked with the river. It was the source of many of my pleasures and sometimes of my sorrows. In it I learned to swim, taught by my father before I can remember; and in summer time I accounted the Saturday afternoon lost if it did not see me by the river with a group of neighborhood boys, often white and black.

Among the latter were almost sure to be Will Long and Edmund Sergeant, both members of families who lived on our place as "croppers." Will was a strong and sturdy boy about five years older than I and always took a protective attitude toward me. I am sure my mother felt, when I was away from the house, that I was safer if I were with Will. Edmund was about my age, perhaps a year older. He was quite black in color and slender in build. He was also timid and biddable, usually ruled by me in all our relationships, which were close and continuous.

It was Edmund with whom I fished in the river and learned most of its lore and all its moods. Edmund and I roamed the woods and fields together in every season. We set out rabbit traps, made by Will and my brother, and rose by break of day in the crisp and frosty mornings to visit those traps and salvage our take. Those were the days of much small game in our area. Rabbits were there in great numbers, though enjoying no benefit of protective laws. Rabbit attained the status of a steady menu on the tables of most farm families, especially the blacks. Edmund and I would often lug home as many as a dozen from our regular before-breakfast visit to our traps. Not our own or our families' need for meat, or liking for rabbit, prompted our continuing campaign against the furry tribe. It was the adventure, the lure of the chase, the old primitive instinct to snare and to hunt. Even now I can recall the tension in my small body as Edmund and I drew toward the site of a trap, and the exaltation in my breast when we saw that the trigger had been sprung and the trap door was down, indicating that a rabbit was likely inside. And yet I found myself often squeamish when I had pulled the uninjured bunny out of the mouth of the box-trap and noted his big and frightened eyes. Occasionally this aversion to the killing was so strong in me that it resulted in a careless holding of the legs, a quick kick by the rabbit, and a consequent uninjured escape. In such instances I never really felt put out as I watched the swiftly disappearing cottontail vanish from sight. Edmund probably rated me careless, but I did not care. If I made vocal explanation it was to myself: "there are plenty more." Subconsciously, however, I knew it was pity, plus a growing tendency to personalize the rabbit. And this grew out of the possession of a treasured book, bought for me by my father. It was *The Tales of Uncle Remus*, by Joel Chandler Harris. In most of the tales Brer Rabbit was the shrewd and spritely hero of the fields and farm, nearly always outwitting the fox, the terrapin, and all the other "varmints" in his neighborhood.

But other and most of the innumerable times at the traps I effected a practical compromise with my feelings by handing the rabbit over to Edmund for the *coup de grâce*. This was administered in either of two ways, both quick and effective. One was to take the captive firmly by the head and, with a quick jerk, break the neck. The other method was to the same end. The rabbit was held suspended by the hind legs and a quick blow at the base of the head with the edge of the hand easily separated the vertebrae of the neck. In either method Edmund was quite expert, the rabbit always being tossed on the ground for his last convulsive kicks. Edmund held it "bad luck" to have him die in his hands.

Our traps for rabbits were of the box variety, about twenty-eight inches long, made of plank about five inches wide. Four pieces were nailed together to make a box. One end was covered. The other end had a slotted door held up by a trigger arrangement made of a uniform stick tied by a string at one end to the top of the door. It ran parallel to the box and was notched in the middle to fit over an eight-inch upright let into the top plank of the box. This upright pivoted the whole arrangement, for at the other end of the stick was tied the trigger proper, which consisted of a thin piece of slot whittled out with a knife and notched near the middle. The lower side of this long notch must needs be cut at right angles with the slot so that it would catch lightly on the edge of an augur hole bored through the top of the box just past its middle length. When the trap was "set" the door was thus held suspended, its lower edge at the top of the slot. When the rabbit entered the open door he was unobstructed until his head touched the two or three inches of the trigger that came down through the hole in the top of the box. This trigger, being touched, dropped the door behind the intruder and he was all snug and comfortable until morning brought Edmund and me on our round of the traps.

There was a deal of art about the construction of traps that does not appear in the brief description above, and a deal of artifice in their successful use after they were made. Curiously, I never learned the art of construction, for I had no need of it. My brother, several years my senior, built all our traps. He could not roam the fields and woods as I, nor swim in the river. He had been stricken with meningitis when he was four years old and never walked normally again. His constant and devoted attendant was the Negro boy, Will, who did his bidding in all things. Will carried him on his back everywhere he went about the place, my brother's arms clasped about Will's neck and his legs gathered under Will's arms. He liked to explore the neighborhood and to exploit its resources in adventure and amusement as well as did Edmund and myself. This he did on Will's back. Often he was at the river with the other boys, though he must needs sit on the bank and watch the others swim and dive. But he could and did fish in the fishing seasons, spending hours by the river with Will in attendance. He and Will gathered more nuts in the fall, and over a wider range, than did Edmund and I. He knew where all the best nut trees were—both hickory and walnut—in the whole area. He and Will would carry a hammer, a tow sack, and a wrapped-up lunch on journeys to distant walnut trees. Arrived at the place of operations, Will would place a flat stone at my brother's hands and then proceed to pick up and pile around him the heavy crop of fallen walnuts that the frosts had yellowed in the pulpy hulls. My brother would work steadily with his hammer and the stone, freeing the nuts from the hulls and accumulating such piles that Will would often have to make return journeys for several days to salvage them all. The nuts served as a winter store at both Will's house and ours, divided in such shares as my brother thought just. But there was plenty for all. We cracked and ate them around our big open fireplace on winter nights, often washed down with persimmon beer.

This beer, too, a delicious and healthful drink, was a product of my brother's management and Will's industry. It was made at our home and the neighboring farms after the following method: A heavy and tightly-hooped molasses barrel was thoroughly washed inside, the heading in one end having been removed. It was set on end upon a platform in a suitable place (at our home, in the "smokehouse") and its bottom and a foot of its inside first lined with clean wheat-straw. Ripe, clean, frost-bitten persimmons shaken off the trees by Will were gathered in quantity and kneaded a bit in a large pan after the manner of bread-dough. Then honey-locust pods were gathered and pummelled in a tub to break them up well.

Along the inner rim of these long flat pods lay a fruit-like pulp of acid sweetness.

These two materials having been properly prepared, a layer of each, some three inches thick, was alternately packed in the barrel with clean straw between the layers. The straw lining was continued up the sides of the barrel as the persimmon and locust layers rose higher. When the barrel was two-thirds full, the mash was covered over with straw and a thin layer of corn meal was sprinkled on top. Then the barrel was filled to the brim with water from the well and the open head covered tightly over. I knew little then, and have learned little since, of chemical processes and the reaction of one substance to another, but I do know that the sparkling golden drink that after two weeks of undisturbed quiet came from the spigot of the barrel was a drink for the gods.

My brother, with Will as servitor, not only brewed the successive barrels of persimmon beer, but took upon himself a great variety of other activities about the place that called for technical skill. He sheared our small flock of sheep with his own skillful hands after the cool spring rains were over. Will, at his orders, would pen the sheep on the chosen day. Will would pinion each animal in succession, lay him before my brother on a suitably low platform and soon his fleece was in the bag. Then the sheep was turned loose to get acquainted with himself without his clothes and another was brought forward by Will. I often sought to relieve his tired hands, but was usually rebuffed on the ground that I was not adroit with the shears and would nip out pieces of skin as I removed the fleece. Probably this would have been true in the beginning stage of my apprenticeship. But he sometimes trusted Will when the dumb sheep was inclined to lie perfectly quiet without the need of special holding. Anyway, Edmund and I never learned to shear a sheep. Once sheep-shearing day fell upon the day of an attack of measles that was discovered by my mother in time to draw my brother into the house and to bed. Even so, by his orders, Will became his substitute and Edmund's and my role through the day was to catch and hold the sheep for Will.

My brother liked carpentry and became quite adept at this industry, with Will to do all the heavier tasks. The two made all our rabbit traps, and they were made with skill and precision. No new timber was utilized in their construction, but old weather-beaten plank was sought out. Theory was that the timid bunny would be afraid of an object that did not blend with the colors of the soil, the dead leaves, and the frost-bitten foliage. I am sure this theory was correct.

The best product of carpentry that came from my brother's hands was a wagon, a goat wagon. The only pleasure we had from it was in the building, the contemplation of its perfection as it stood when finished. It was two feet high and twice as long. Its wheels were in exact imitation of buggy wheels, each spoke whittled out in perfect proportion and set in the rims tightly bound with tires. Procuring the tires and tightening them on had been the main problem. But this had been solved by the collaboration of the Negro blacksmith at the country store and post office. The wheels and chassis were of oak throughout. The bed, or body, was pine. All were painted red, the only color we had available. This wagon was undoubtedly a work of art when finished and had cost my brother and Will many a day in the making. Edmund and I had quite a period of time to admire it since harness for the goat had to be provided after the wagon was complete. This was made from a calf skin, tanned at the local tannery and donated by my father. I had held the goat for measurements and had wondered at the time if his wicked soul could be confined.

The goat was mine, my individual property—all I owned besides two dogs and a runty pig. He had been given to me as a bleating kid by Mr. Joe Thaxton, an admirer of my second oldest sister. I had raised him without much effort or extra care. He was a self-reliant goat from the beginning and never developed any morals. When his early little new-moon horns had grown into great curving hooks that spread out from his head, when he had grown a six-inch beard and learned to chew tobacco, then he was a wholly self-confident beast that tended to dominate the barnlot. He dominated the timid sheep. He had a special peeve against the ram. He pushed the cows around and chased the calves like a fiend possessed. Even our dogs would walk out of his way, with wary watching against his charge. He loved to rear on his hindlegs and walk like a man. He was a satyr in appearance and largely in action. Once he invaded our living room through a door left open by the careless cook. Table was set for dinner, with all the food on. The cook attempted to eject him with a chair as weapon. The goat, not to be intimidated, bounded upon the table and whirled about from end to end to defend himself. It reproduced with trimmings the tale of the fabled bull in the china shop. Had my father been at home I think this would have been the last day of Billy. Even so, it left a heavy black mark upon his reckless record.

It was this animal, castrated and with the ends of his horns sawed off, that we proposed to reduce to a beast of burden. We would hitch him to the beautiful red wagon and he would trundle my brother about in partial relief of Will. The day came when the harness was all complete. My brother sat on the ground near by to supervise. Edmund brought out the wagon from the woodshed. I had haltered Billy and brought him up from the barnlot. He seemed indifferent while Will put on the harness. Even when he was put into the shafts, and all was hooked up, he continued to chew his cud with only one contemplative "blah."

The question arose as to who should drive first. My brother leaned toward Will, but I argued him out of it. I held that he was my goat, that I even ought to charge for his services. I pointed out that the goat would "mind" me better—though I knew this to be weak and spurious argument. Anyway I won the point and was elected to drive. I think perhaps my brother was swayed by my hint of future charges for goat-service. He was a very shrewd trader.

The point settled, I mounted the wagon, sitting flat in the bed with my feet extending forward to the front end. It was a very nice fit. I had tried it numbers of times before this day. Will handed me the lines (reins) and stepped aside. Edmund said "watch out," but I was quite confident and shouted to the goat to "git up." He did, for a pace or two, as calmly as you please. Then he stopped. Edmund handed me a switch. I tapped out a light blow across his erect tail. The imp now bolted with the speed of a cannonball. He pointed straight for the gate of the barnlot. This gate I had left part-way open when I had first led out the goat. Now I rued the day. The gate was open plenty wide for the goat, even perhaps for the wagon—if care had been taken. I saw impending disaster. I vaguely heard shouts of my brother to "Stop 'im!" But this was quite impossible and I knew it. Some ten feet from the gate I abandoned the meteor and rolled off on the sliding ground. I heard a loud crash but I paid little mind. I was holding a blood-spurting nose and was sure my arm was broken. The wagon now amounted to mere kindling wood when Will gathered it up at the gate, from which the goat had gone on. Only two wheels on one side seemed to remain whole. My brother blamed me and was in a rage. Edmund, ever my loyal servitor, piped up weakly to the effect that "de Debil himself couldn't stop dat goat when he wants to go!"

The wagon was never rebuilt and the goat never harnessed again. He lived a carefree life and took to roaming with the cattle when they were turned out in the fall to roam in common and browse upon the leavings of crops in the river bottoms. This brought him to a tragic end. He was set upon by a pack of mongrel dogs belonging to Negroes on the Williams place. I knew it was these dogs because I found a dead one not far from where I found the skeleton of the goat. This fact, plus further evidence of crippled dogs around the Negroes' cabins, led me to know that Demon Billy had gone down fighting. I salvaged his beard, which the hungry dogs and buzzards had left intact. For long it hung as a souvenir on a nail in the woodshed by the useless harness and the two sound red wheels.

The "setting" and "tending" of the traps my brother made fell to Edmund's and my lot, and in this we became quite expert—what with the effective traps my brother kept provided. All the ways of the rabbit we picked up naturally. Their paths were located by us, their "gnaws" on fence-rails where they habitually passed through, and the persimmon trees where they visited in the night to eat the freshly-fallen and frost-sweetened persimmons (Edmund and I always called them "simmons"). We learned that the rabbit did not enter a box-trap by lure of any kind of "bait," either of apple core, bits of turnip, or other vegetable tidbits. His instinct was that of a burrowing animal. He entered the door of the trap to explore for a snug burrow away from the sharp chill of the frosts. This we learned by reason of the fact that our "take" was always larger on a very cold morning, when the river bottoms and the hillsides were covered with a hoar frost. We usually did "bait" one trap, slightly larger than the usual rabbit trap. But this was for opossums ("possum" to me). This trap must be set at the base of a persimmon tree, where the opossum repaired at night for his fill of this delectable fruit. But the opossum is a coarse feeder and more fond of offal than even of choice ripe fruit. Hence our bait for opossum was apt to be the entrails of a drawn chicken, placed in the very back end of the trap where the opossum, lured by the smell, was sure to spring the trigger in his search for the food. Once caught, an opossum, to be prepared for the table, must needs be confined for a period of two or three weeks and fed on clean food to rid his system of his previous diet. Then, properly roasted and his excessive fat rendered out, he makes a dish for the epicure. At our house he was always served on a large platter with juicy sweet potatoes ranged around. All our family of eight except one fastidious sister enjoyed a possum dinner.

Not only did we make war on Brer Rabbit with traps but we kept two or three rabbit dogs, of mixed ancestry, with which we hunted at all seasons except spring and summer. These dogs, joined to those of other boys in the neighborhood, made many a field-day of my childhood activities. No guns were allowed by our elders in these rabbit hunts. We chased our prey down with dogs and our own strategy. I was eleven years old before my father allowed me to have a gun, and then over my anxious mother's protest. It was a single-barrel breechloader without great range or carrying power. But I thought of it as in the class with artillery and became the envy of all my companions. I cleaned it carefully, inside and out, after each hunt and reserved it mainly for partridges, which I began to hunt. This gun soon made me ambitious to own a bird dog and this I acquired in the form of an English setter pup which I named Nick.

Our area was full of quail in that period, despite the fact that there were as yet no game laws. Netting was still a favorite way of taking quail and no one yet held it to be unsportsmanlike. Netting was done on horses. Riders would course the stubble fields at a slow walk, watching closely on every side. When a covey of birds was located the rider, or riders, drew off to an appropriate distance so as not to flush the birds. Then the long barrel net was taken from its cover beside the saddle. This net was some fifteen feet long and was made of stout knotted threads and kept circular in shape by small white oak hoops that diminished in size from the mouth of the net to the closed other end. The open end hoop was a curved wicket whose sharpened ends were stuck in the ground when the collapsible net was stretched out to be set. At the small closed end of the net a wooden peg was attached. This peg was stuck in the ground when the net was set, and held it rigid. The wings of the net were made detached. They were two in number, made of similar netting about twelve inches wide and twelve feet long. This netting was attached to straight small stakes with sharpened ends to stick in the ground. When the barrel of the net had been staked out at quite a distance from the covey of birds, and in the direction they seemed inclined to go, then the wings were staked out from the mouth of the net in the form of the letter V. After a bit of dead weeds or grass had been thrown upon the top of the wicket the riders mounted and began the "drive." This was a slow and ofttimes tedious process and required many a turning and twisting of your horse, many a retreat and advance to prevent the birds' taking flight. But it was the instinct of the birds to group when slightly alarmed and run in the cover away from the twisting horsemen. And so after a while they were driven into the wings of the V and ran along its sides until they entered the barrel and down its course until they were one scrambling mass at its small end. In the meantime the rider dismounted and pulled up the wicket to close the mouth.

This system of taking birds is now fortunately against the mores of sportsmanship and is fittingly prohibited by modern game laws. But it was a custom of the country from early colonial times until the end of the eighteenth century. And with all the many reasons for its disappearance let no man suppose that the technical skill and the knowledge of quail habits required in their netting was second in any degree to that of the sportsman who shoots over dogs in the approved customs of the present time. This netting of birds was one form of hunting my brother could do. He could sit a horse and he was patient, a quality which this activity required in definite degree. He on his horse and Will on a mule, with the netting equipment attached, they would ride the fields all day long. Will handled the net under my brother's instructions when birds had been found. But he himself did the driving. They would return sometimes with over half a hundred quail, and so lavish was our supply of birds that no one thought of them as a delicacy. In the fall of the year we had this game on the table far more frequently than chicken.

My brother's hunting impulse was not wholly satisfied with bird netting. At times he rode rabbit hunting, with Will and the rest of the boys all on foot with the hounds. Occasionally, without a "by your leave," he borrowed my dearly prized gun and went off on Will's back to the nearest timbered area for squirrels. Still-hunting is the most effective method with squirrels, and for this my brother was qualified in his incapacity to walk. He would have Will make the approach quietly and place him in a sheltered position adjacent to hickory-nut trees where the squirrels came for their present needs and their winter store. Here the two would wait out the suspicions of twittering tree-flitting birds—jays, nuthatches, and downy woodpeckers. Then the squirrels would begin to gather in the nut trees. Only favorable shots could be chosen by my brother, this predicated upon the limitations of my single-barrel short-range gun. He must kill at his first shot, or lose his game, for the squirrel is a wily little beast and tenacious of life. Once he mounted Will's back for a more favorable position at a wounded bushy-tail and in his zeal shot from this position at the moving target. The action was unexpected by Will and quite discomforting. I noticed thereafter that Will would incline to make other proposals for roving, and claim it was not a good day for squirrels—that the leaves were too dry, or the wind too high.

Then perhaps we would go fishing instead. The river ran, with many a crook and turn, through the hills of our place. Some of the best fishing holes were down the stream several miles from us, where the tributary Little Duck which flowed through the Winstead lands, joined our river, the Hyco. That side of our place was contained in a great fenced pasture, where our cattle, our hogs, and a small flock of sheep were kept. This pasture was more than a mile across and fenced with heavy split rails of oak where it passed through the woods in its northern half. The more open part was fenced with wire of the barbed variety to force the respect of the cattle, especially the bull.

My father had bought a Jersey male yearling to make a beginning in "grading up" our cattle. He said we would have more milk from purer bred cows. This Will and I deprecated, for it fell to our lot to milk four cows both night and morning. But there were pigs to feed, and buttermilk was an excellent diet for pigs. Often I leaned on the fence of the pigpen and watched young porkers swill a trough of milk that Will and I, with cramping hands, had drained so tediously from the udders of the cows.

Our young bull had grown into a mighty beast when I was ten years old and he was five. He commanded respect in the pasture and from the Negroes about the barnlot. A heavy log pen had now been built down back of the barn for his especial keep. This pen was twenty feet square with a shed in a corner for weather protection. Here neighbors' cows were brought to visit our bull. But even so the confinement seemed to sour his temper and he grew more and more unruly. It became a standing order of my father that children keep away from the bull pen. This order we obeyed without exception and the beast was not now let out to pasture with the cows. He was fed and watered by a Negro man, named Rafe, Uncle Calvin's oldest son and Edmund's brother. Rafe carried a pitchfork if he had occasion to enter the pen.

Even so my mother constantly worried about some possible miscarriage in the handling of the bull and pleaded with my father to be rid of him. She even ordered my brother and Will and Edmund and me to keep out of the pasture, into which the bull would escape if he broke out of his pen. Our one flouting of this order led to near tragedy, and is one of the most deeply printed memories of my childhood.

My brother on Will's back, with Edmund and me carrying fishing poles and a pail of lunch, went for a day's fishing down the river about two miles distance near the mouth of the Little Duck. Through the pasture was the most direct route to our goal. But, going, we traveled much out of our way around the outside of the pasture fence and thus lost some of our fishing time. Yet we had a good day, lingering at the river later than we should as late evening came on. The fish seemed to bite better at this stage of the day and perhaps this beguiled us. Anyway, we started late from the river and came direct to the pasture fence. Should we circle it, as we had in coming, or should we push straight through in disregard of mother's orders? My brother, always indulged by our parents and something of a law unto himself, made the decision. Perhaps he thought of Will, upon whose back he rode. Certainly he reasoned that the bull was secure in his pen, and even the cows now gone home and gathered about the barn. At any rate his decision was to cross the pasture, and none of us felt very guilty in the act.

We were probably half way across, and moving fast, when an ominous sound broke upon the air. It was the wild and far-reaching cry of the bull raised in mating call to all cows in a radius of miles. We had heard it many times from the bull in his pen and we knew all its wild nuances. But the thing that struck terror in our breasts was the fact that this piercing elk-like call was not from the direction of the barn and bull pen.

It came from toward the right, the wooded part of the pasture. It was proof that the beast was out and on the rampage. Was he moving in our direction? How far off was he? Could Will with the burden of my brother on his back reach the home side of the pasture in time? These questions were quickly answered. The bull raised his voice again in a low and rumbling thunder quite unlike his first lilting and high-held bugle note. He was coming in our direction, and fast! We could now hear the pounding of his feet as he made through the scrub and a few sparse trees in this part of the pasture. The timid Edmund promptly took to the nearest tree and was full twelve feet up when the bull hove in sight. All that held me to the ground was a subconscious necessity to fend for my brother and the panting Will. Will was now running in the direction of home and almost as if he carried no weight.

I had stopped still, half-frozen in my tracks. The bull had also stopped for a moment, as if to survey the scene. Then he let out another thunderous rumble and half turned to the fleeing Will. At that moment I screamed from the depth of my body out of sheer terror of the impending charge upon Will. I was nearest the bull by considerable yardage. I had lost ground in my indecision over whether to follow Edmund up his tree or to stick by my brother and Will. My wild scream now brought the bull's head around sharply to me. He started for me with lowered head. His starting point, Edmund's tree, and myself made a triangle, the shortest leg being from myself to the tree. This proved my immediate salvation. I could not and did not reason, but instinct whipped me out of my tracks and toward the tree. This, too, I knew I hadn't time to climb, but it seemed to offer refuge. It did, for the moment. The bull swerved as I ran, but I reached the tree and packed my body behind it at the very moment his huge bulk hurtled by so close that his side rattled the bark in an inch of my face. The momentum of his charge carried him some thirty paces past. I have always felt he might have kept on in the direction he was headed had not Edmund, perched safely above in the fork of the tree, now begun to screech at the top of his lungs. Edmund's caterwauling caused the bull to turn when his momentum was spent, by which time I was halfway up the tree and making rapid progress toward Edmund's position much higher up. Here a happy diversion occurred, happy for us, in our grandstand seat, and humiliating, even belittling to the bull.

My dog, Sport, had arrived on the scene. Sport was a three-year-old mongrel I had acquired when he was a puppy from the litter of a bitch owned by a thriftless Negro family on Captain Robert Williams' place just across the river from ours. I had brought this puppy home and faced my father with a *fait accompli*. My father had reluctantly consented to my keeping him, but on condition that I assume full responsibility. This I had done, and the puppy had grown into full doghood and was devoted to me. Often I had speculated about the blood stream of Sport, and what strain predominated. Certainly he had some shepherd blood because he was effective as help in driving the cows and penning the sheep. He would also point birds in an indifferent way; and rabbits he chased by sight, but never by scent. He was an active fellow, though not inclined to trouble with the other dogs. He liked to follow me everywhere and usually did unless forbidden. The day of our fishing and our adventure with the bull, Sport had been left at home at the insistence of my brother because he would (according to my brother) scare off the fish by swimming in the water or running up and down the bank. I had reluctantly yielded to this reasoning and left the dog watching our departure, looking despondent and disappointed.

Now, with Edmund and me treed by the bull, Sport had come to the rescue. My theory is that he first learned of the escape of the bull from his pen and his rumbling movement into the wide pasture spaces. The dog's curiosity must have led him into investigation in that direction. He was probably drawing nearer when my first loud cry rang out over the hills. And now he was here at the very moment the bull turned after the charge that so narrowly missed me at the tree.

Sport now took charge of the situation. He proved himself a wily and judicious matador. He was an in-and-out fighter; always he struck from behind, with a quick gnash or nip on hock or heel or tail of the ponderous brute. The bull would whirl and Sport would be on the other side, away. He would circle and dart, and always the bull would know he had been in, though now he was out. It was a pretty sight from my perch in the tree. Even Edmund had gained confidence and grown quiet, watching with me the skilled manoeuvering of Sport. A faint "Sic em!" now and then was our only contribution.

Sport's ultimate proof of strategy finally developed into a change of tactics. He had fought silently in his slash-and-get-away attacks on the rear. This had kept the bull whirling and thrashing about, but was doing no real harm to the beast or routing him from the field of battle. The dog now moved to the front, never too close, and began to bark and growl. He defied the bull to come on. The bull would make his charge and Sport would dart aside as he went by and was soon in front again for a repetition of the manoeuver. This process he repeated again and again until the bull became saturated with disgust. He was now some seventy-five yards distant from our tree where Sport had led his successive futile charges. The sequel was that at this point came the clear notes in the amorous call of a lowing cow from across the hills toward the river. The bull threw up his head in the very face of one of the dog's dares and answered the cow in his own love challenge. Then he began to trot away in the direction of the cow. Sport let him go without further ado, as if to say, "Well, that's that!"

Will came up just after the bull disappeared. I inquired about my brother and found that Will had handed him up in a tree of low-growing branches not far from the home side of the pasture, where he was waiting for Will's return. I now climbed down, and Edmund also, after some hesitation and another long look to insure himself against the bull's return. We hastened across to my brother, soon had him down from his tree, and made a quick run of the short remaining distance home. We met Rafe and a helper, both with pitchforks, starting out in search of the bull. They inquired if we had seen the bull. All we said was "Yes, and he went that way!"

Rafe returned at dark and reported to my father that the bull had broken through the fence and gone across the hills, perhaps had crossed the river. Next day, he was found, in mellower mood, in company with a cow from a neighboring farm. With much help Rafe drove him home, with the cow alongside to make him tractable. Our experience in the pasture now came out, though we had conspired to keep it secret. Soon father took early steps to have the beast slaughtered and sold to a butcher in our county town.

But my memory of him has remained keen through the years —the clear and glistening yellow of his sides and hinder parts, the brown laid-on-yellow from the saddle forwards, including the head. Even lingers, from that far-off day, the echo of the the challenge in his high-calling love note as it rang out over the hills and the valley of the river where my early memories cluster.

As time went on and I grew up to about twelve, a gradual change took place that brought me in as substitute for Will in his pack-horse relations to my brother—except on special occasions. It occurred so gradually that I, at the time, seemed not to have noticed the happening, certainly offered no question or sought any definite reason therefor. I think I even accepted the shift with pride, pride that I was grown so strong. Also, though my brother was nearly four years my senior, he was not my weight when I had reached twelve years. His height as well as weight was a full third less than normal for his age. Looking back I seem also to remember, too, and well now I know, that those years were all hard years for country families, both white and black. Will was needed more in the fields, in the planting of corn and tobacco and in their cultivation and harvesting. His father, Joe, wished this his eldest and most capable son to take his place in the crop. Though Will was not lazy I recall that he grouched a bit at the change of employment, for he was fond of my brother and seemed to think the latter's interests would suffer.

But the change came about and was already adjusted without special planning. I seem to have adjusted more readily than did my brother. Doubtless this was due to my great willingness to "tote" him about on my back, but with notions of my own as to where we should go and what we should do. If he wanted to go for hickory nuts in the woods I might urge a fishing trip on the river. He usually got his way but ofttimes not without argument. Will had been always acquiescent—except possibly in the case of shooting squirrels from his back. But me he sometimes likened to Balaam's ass for the reason that I talked back to my rider.

Once we had a strange and puzzling experience, one that stands out in my memory today in even sharper outline than our brush with the bull. Our mother had sent us on an errand—to take a tin bucket of butter to Miss Betsy Boyd, who lived the life of a recluse in a cabin on my Uncle's place about a mile distant from our home. Miss Betsy was a strange person who had come into our neighborhood from unknown parts. She was accompanied by an old-maid daughter who became a sewing woman "by the day" for the families about. She returned to her mother in the late evenings, but all the rest of the time Miss Betsy dwelt alone and in season cultivated a small garden.

Much of the time she poked about on a hobble-stick, looking very much like a witch with her bent carriage and always in dark clothes and a slatted poke-bonnet.

My mother knew her life to be bare and poverty-stricken. Sometimes she sent her things by the daughter, Miss Jenny, when the latter sewed a day or two at our house. Other times she sent by whatever carriage offered. If none did, she (at irregular intervals) sent Will and my brother. Now she sent my brother and me, cautioning him to let me rest if I got tired. I was confident, however, since the distance was only a mile each way. So we set off, the bucket in my brother's hands and bumping a bit in my tummy as I pushed along the overgrown path. Nearly at Miss Betsy's house, and in full sight, I halted a bit to "blow." Glancing casually around I saw the old woman some fifty yards distant across a slight ravine and on the slope of the opposite hill. My brother also noted her at the same time and said she was gathering wild plums. We observed her for a moment leaning on her stick and reaching for the fruit with her other hand. Then my brother called. Immediately, in the self-same moment, she wasn't there. Then we turned in wonder toward the cabin. Miss Betsy was standing in its open door. The breath went out of me. I could barely whisper, "Let's go back."

Already I was turning on wobbling knees when my brother said, "But Miss Betsy needs the butter." I eased the pail out of his hand, letting one of his useless legs dangle. I sidled toward a pine stump that stood by the path and set the pail thereon. Then I whispered, "You watch while I travel." I made fast time back the way we came, my strength picking up in proportion to the distance from Miss Betsy's house. We were in sight of home when my brother observed that a witch couldn't hurt us in broad open daytime. I was not so sure and so was glad and exhausted when we reached our backyard gate. Only then did I feel secure.

Our mother laughed at our trembling-told tale and said we had been listening to too many of Puss's (the cook's) ghost stories. But we both had seen her, and we *knew* we had! I can see her today, as clearly as then—over fifty years ago. And my brother who lived a long and useful life never had a moment's doubt of our version of the facts. We spoke of it sometimes in after years, and both of us were ever beyond question in the faith that Miss Betsy on that occasion was either in two places at once or else abridged the distance of one hundred yards in the bat of an eye. In the meantime Miss Betsy continued to have our mother's gifts, but she received them by other conveyance than ourselves. We never ventured to her cabin again. In fact Edmund and I removed all our traps from that side of the farm, though it was good trapping ground. Edmund, who had been told the facts by me, expressed my own definite convictions. He said, "Miss Betsy sholy is a witch"; and, "I wonders can she cunjer us by jes looking?" Anyway, we didn't propose to give her much chance.

Our Two Captains

In the rural countryside where I was born, religious denominations were inextricably mixed. Though all were Protestant, of one brand or another, and consciously held that all other segments of religious faith were error, there was great toleration within the common bond of Protestantism. True, there were shades of difference in the credos of Methodists, Baptists, Presbyterians, and Episcopalians, but these differences were not made fighting issues in the general Christian body. The label of one or the other of these four churches, or their subdivisions, made the individual respectable and worthy of consideration. The Methodists were strongest in percentage of the population, the Baptists second, the Presbyterians third, and Episcopalians quite rare. In their reactions to religion the first three groups were typical of the "Bible Belt," a characterization much later applied to the whole Southland of somewhat indefinite boundaries. Our few Episcopalians were held to be, and doubtless were, more liberal in Bible interpretation and more tolerant of "sin."

Sin in the common view had tended to lose its original meaning of the quality of an act and came to connote living out of formal relation with any church. If you were in or of a church, any of our churches, you were a Christian. If out of this relation, you were a sinner. It was constantly incumbent upon the good Christian to save the sinners by inducing them into the fold of church membership. The sinner was the unsaved, the unredeemed, and if he died in that unholy state his fate was damnation in another world. If he accepted the bond of fellowship in a church without hypocrisy, then he was saved. This distinction between the status of men was real enough in community consciousness to make of it a compelling force.

It was inculcated by the clergy and accepted by the laity. It made for discipline in social conduct and was a vocal pressure in the annual week of religious revivals in most of the churches. An individual who isolated himself from the formal organization, who did not attend church, was bothered not at all. He was merely subject to the assumption that he was an irregular and took his own risk.

Several of the elders in my community when I was a boy did just that. Two I hold in mind with particular memory. They were Captain Robert Williams and Captain Robert Sergeant, both ex-soldiers of the Civil War and both then growing old in their several ways. Doubtless the reason for my interest arose out of propinquity. Captain Robert Williams' place adjoined ours on the east, just across the river. Captain Sergeant's on our side of the river adjoined on the south. These two men, old men to me, were quite unlike in quality and character. And yet they shared fundamental characteristics of close similarity. These were three in the main. Both were ex-slaveholders, ex-soldiers, and non-conformists in the matter of any creed or church. To these similarities may be added an addiction to drink, an overpowering habit in the case of both. Yet they never foregathered, never drank together, and were practically strangers to each other, though living only two miles apart. Even their lands adjoined a mile up the river from our home. I recall no single instance of any intercourse whatever between them. Nor do I believe this stemmed from any active enmity or past incident in their lives. Rather I sensed then and continue to believe that some innate quality of difference in what we term men's "souls" accounted for their calm indifference to each other's existence. Probably their drinking habits had a different meaning to each—for there was a difference in both method and result.

Captain Sergeant would get drunk at considerable intervals; Captain Williams as often as he could find the means, and in this he was always quite adroit. Captain Sergeant's liquor sharpened his wit and spruced up his good manners to the point of courtliness. It stimulated his zest for music and his love of poetry. In his cups he would visit preferred neighbors unasked, playing his accordion up and down the road, probably fancying himself a troubadour. Likely, too, he would bear in a pocket a volume of Scott, or his copy of Burns to press as a loan upon some member of the visited household.

He had been one of the many who had come back from the battles of northern Virginia to find their old world gone. All was wreck and ruin where once there had been a way of life to which most had adjusted and many had found a satisfying order. Social organization had been stable and at the top of this agrarian order a confident culture was arising. But political forces, followed by the crash of arms, had toppled all this over. The immediate problem was to live. Deep discouragement at one end of the social scale, wild hope at the other, characterized the post-bellum picture. But even among the broken there were those who girded their loins for the tasks of adjustment, for the building of a new structure on the wreckage of the old. But many of that generation never gathered the courage. Their old world was dead. They were shaped for that world and fitted for no other. Why not live out their span in just dreaming, deadening the pains of life as best one might?

Captain Robert Sergeant was of this type. He possessed a good estate in well-wooded land, a quarter of the old Sergeant property, lying on the slopes of the hills to the west of the river and just south of my father's home. His share and that of another brother named James had apparently been set off from the old Sergeant estate when they had reached maturity. An older brother, Uncle John, and their sister, Cousin Delphia, had remained at the old home, their shares undivided. Captain Robert was unmarried when he went off to the war and of course returned in the same single state. Neither he, nor any member of his family had ever labored with their hands on the soil. His body and his tastes made him quite unfit for this sort of life. The scattered and disorganized ex-slaves were quite unready for a healthy beginning in their new status of freemen. Captain Robert developed no skill in management under these circumstances. For full two decades after the Civil War he had a bare subsistence from the meagre returns of a succession of landless white tenants. Then he finally made a venture as country merchant at a crossroads store. Here he did better and tended to prosper in a small way. He adopted the sound principle, in his own lack of capital, of no credit to his customers and he was scrupulously honest with his own creditors for stock of trade. He was always courteous and dignified and commanded full respect, both at his "store" and among all his acquaintance. This was true though it was community-wide knowledge that his bane was drink.

Too young myself to properly evaluate, I nevertheless sensed the community appraisal of Captain Robert Sergeant. It was wholly tolerant and understanding. To his contemporaries of the same generation he was a person who would have adorned the order of a generation now past, a generation in which the families of the better sort had property and leisure and a sense of security. This order had passed, leaving many of its representatives with no heart for rebuilding. To live out your days like the gentleman you were was now quite impossible. That which is honor in an inward sense the Captain had. He was a man whose word you would take without thought or question. He could have lived on promises, for years at least, but never did. His drinking became immoderate as the years went by but in his cups he was quite genteel in his speech and manners. There seemed no coarseness in his soul. He was never profane or boisterous. He had a courtly bow for his friends, bending slightly from his waist as he tipped his hat; non-acquaintances he passed by in apparent unawareness of their existence. I think no one would have slapped him on the back even when loaded to the gunnels with drink. Neatness and cleanliness characterized his well-worn clothes. This puzzled many people when they thought on his poverty. But to our family the explanation was clear. Aunt Harriet and Uncle Calvin, former slaves of the Sergeants, lived on our place as croppers for some twenty years. They never lost interest in and loyalty to the Sergeants. They made a monthly Sunday visit to the old Sergeant house, where Uncle John and Cousin Delphia lived. Captain Robert's bachelor home was just adjoining. So Aunt Harriet made it her duty and pleasure to see that his clothes requirements were met. This was done without parade or advertisement and as a labor of love. She would send one of her boys back and forth each week to Captain Robert's place, bearing worn but immaculate shirts on their return with other fresh clothes. We made no doubt that new clothes, provided by Aunt Harriet herself, were often placed with them, and probably without Captain Robert's notice.

Thus he kept up a fundamental of gentility, pleasing to himself and a silent and secret pride to Aunt Harriet. I recall an incident that particularly impressed this clothes relation upon my memory. I was dropping in with Edmund at Aunt Harriet's cabin hoping for a piece of ash-cake at Aunt Harriet's hands. She was talking to Uncle Calvin as she examined a torn and dirty suit of old clothes she had taken from a bundle which Rafe, her son, had just brought from the Captain's place. The Captain's liquor had nauseated him, a fact to which these clothes bore abundant evidence. They were spread on the cabin floor and Aunt Harriet was looking them over with pained disgust. I heard her remark to Uncle Calvin: "I do wish Marse Robert could tote his likker a little bit better." I was sure Edmund and I were not supposed to hear, so we went out in embarrassment and without the ash-cake.

Captain Robert Sergeant's love for music forms a distinctive part of my memory of him. Whether he had had any training in this art in his boyhood days before the Civil War I do not know. His then stable economic and social position could have made it easily possible. Yet he may have been self-taught, a product of a deep love for music and a sense for rhythm. The violin (we called it fiddle) and the accordion were his favorite instruments. He was quite proficient with both. I have heard in my youth that he played the violin when sober and the accordion when drunk. Upon invitation he would visit neighbors' houses and bring his violin in its case and play many selections at request from young and old. He would come after supper on summer evenings. No particular formality accompanied these visits, but at my home we would have chairs on the lawn and under the trees; perhaps a few neighbors would have dropped in. Captain Robert would chat a while with our elders and then begin to play.

From what in later years I heard some of his contemporaries say, he must have had a little acquaintance with classical music; but the music he served out to such audiences as ours was the popular variety. The pieces were likely to be by Stephen Foster, then in great vogue, or other southern airs of nostalgic quality. To these he added a repertoire of airs of Scotland, and some of Ireland. Most of these were short poems of Burns set to music that have held their charm down through the years. "Annie Laurie" was a favorite of both the musician and the auditors. "Flow Gently Sweet Afton" enjoyed high favor, along with "Coming Through the Rye." Moore's "The Last Rose of Summer" came in for great acclaim.

Captain Robert never essayed to accompany his music with song. Yet he did a thing that to us was almost as effective. He had a great memory for verse, and before each piece he played he rendered a verse or two in words, together with the refrain. He did this particularly with his Burns, for he dearly loved that poet. In the Foster songs there was scarce need, for most of that generation knew these well. "Darling Nelly Gray" and "Love's Old Sweet Song" were also among the favorites always called for. To me, to this day, the songs Captain Robert played are the essence of music.

The picture in my mind of the Captain and his music at our house carries clearly with it the presence of Aunt Harriet and Uncle Calvin and most of their family of boys. When it was known that the Captain was coming, these two old slaves of the Sergeant family would be notified. Aunt Harriet would come up to our kitchen in the afternoon and make a great cake and perhaps ice cream, when ice was available. When the musician arrived after supper her group would appear, perhaps minus Rafe, the eldest son, who was likely to be off on his own romantic concerns. The elders would greet "Marse Robert." He would bow from the waist and then shake hands with both Uncle Calvin and Aunt Harriet, often patting the latter on the cheek with his hand. This ceremony seemed quite natural to all the company.

When the music was over, Aunt Harriet, with help of her own selection, began the service of the cake and ice cream, or cool lemonade. It was ritual that she served my mother first, and then Marse Robert. My father came next, then all lesser people, finally getting down to Edmund and me. If more than several neighbors were present, either old or young, I was usually afraid the cake would be all gone before I was served. And I have seen Aunt Harriet serve the Captain twice before my time came.

Captain Robert's romantic vein found other expression than in his poetry and music, though closely bound up with these. He paid court to the ladies in a discriminating sort of way. For a number of years he visited Miss Willie Lea, of Leasburg, a very small village about five miles distant from our home. Miss Willie was near Captain Robert's age and taught music and other subjects in her father's private school for girls. Their music was a bond, their manners and tastes had been molded by the same ante-bellum environment. But the romance never matured. Perhaps Captain Robert's lack of the material things to make a home was a factor. But the story ran that his habit of drink destroyed his prospects.

I fancy the Captain's hopes were near their sunset on the occasion of his call upon the lady one moonlit summer evening. The story ran that she was waiting on her porch behind a covering trellis rose. She saw the Captain, weaving an uncertain course along the sidewalk to her gate at the foot of the flower-bordered walk. Over-long fumbling with the familiar gate-latch gave definite proof of the Captain's state. Miss Willie's voice, in notes of quavering despair, came across the lawn: "Please, Captain, *do* not come in. I am *afraid* of you!" The Captain stiffened, stepped back, lifted his hat and, bowing from the waist, replied: "Yes, lady, and I am afraid of you, too!" Then, with almost military precision, the Captain straightened and marched away.

Later, when this pale romance had been finished several years, the Captain singled out as the object of his regard a most attractive woman much younger than himself. He was now near sixty and had had a little success in his latest years as a country merchant. His heart now turned toward a cousin of mine, a niece of my mother's, less than half his age. He in no way made himself or the young lady conspicuous in pressing his suit; but he sought her out by visits to her home. Cousin Henrietta was tall and blond, with hair that shone like gold. This she kept meticulously, with never a strand out of place. Her face was like a cameo, so clearly was it chiseled. But with all her grace and loveliness of person she had never found a suitor that her mother, strong-minded Aunt Anne didn't rebuff. Hence Captain Robert's attention to Cousin Henrietta was doomed to no fruitage from the start. His lack of fortune and his well-known habit of drink, plus the added handicap of disparity in age, were factors too important to be ignored by my practical Aunt Anne.

So this heart-hope of the Captain had to wither not long after its birth. And in a year Cousin Henrietta herself died, of a natural cause, and was buried amid the trees in the neighborhood churchyard (Concord). Here, I have been told, by those I believed, Captain Robert would repair in his cups on moonlit nights in summertime, and play by Cousin Henrietta's grave America's best-loved song of that time, "Listen to the Mocking Bird." The cadence of all its notes I know and the best of its lines:

> I am dreaming now of Hallie, Sweet Hallie.
> She's sleeping in the Valley,
> And the mocking-bird is singing where she lies.
>
> *Chorus*
>
> Listen to the mocking-bird,
> Listen to the mocking-bird,
> The mocking-bird still singing o'er her grave.
> Listen to the mocking-bird,
> Listen to the mocking-bird,
> Still singing where the weeping willows wave.

Captain Robert Williams I knew far better than Captain Robert Sergeant. I had a closer view by actual association and much contact. He loved the outdoors at all seasons. He fished and trapped the river and was far more companionable to a growing boy. Admittedly he was far more wicked than Captain Sergeant. He got drunk oftener. He was loud and boisterous when drinking and given to profanity. He was much less mannerly and courteous in behavior, sober or drunk. Before my memory began, his lovely wife had died in poverty, he at her bedside drunk as a lord and bemoaning his future lorn state. These things the whole community knew, and sometimes my elders adverted to them when Captain Williams lived on for many years in ever-increasing demoralization. His morale was all gone when I grew up to be conscious of him as living in the large old house across the river on the hill opposite ours.

He had a son, John, as carefree as himself and also defiant of sober opinion. The Captain went his own way, John went his, and so did the farm—all downhill. But of this I was scarcely aware at the time, for the place and its occupants came to interest me increasingly. It was different somehow. It had been a fine place in slaveowning days, though probably then rather badly managed. The house was large and stately, a long porch in front with attic pillars gave it an hospitable air. Enough paint lingered on to mark its earlier state. On the left end a second porch came out, half length, but in no way destroying the symmetry of the whole. No L extension disfigured the back. A kitchen and store-room were some twenty-five paces from the house on that side. This had been the custom in an older day when slaves were owned and service no problem. It also decreased the hazard of fire. My own and most other homes in my community preserved this feature, long years after the days of slavery.

The Williams house was particularly notable for its site and for the old trees that still lingered on the scene. It faced the west from its seat on a gentle knoll which itself was the crest of a ridge. The ridge was the backbone of land that ran northward between the Hyco River and its tributary Little Duck before they joined below the Winstead Place. The view to the west was across the valley of the river and toward our house on an opposite ridge. The eastward view was across the

Little Duck toward the Big Woods. The old slave quarters, or the remnants thereof were on this side, down the slope from the back of the kitchen. Here all was dilapidation and decay. No renewals had occurred since slavery days, now a quarter of a century past. But the Negroes were numerous and lived in squalor. Dogs rivaled in number the little black children. The families seemed to fend for themselves, with no authority or direction from Captain Bob or his son John. Some had thrown up small pine log cabins at convenient spots more distant from the home place. Cultivation was in little patches scattered about at random. Old broken-down stock of both horses and mules pulled a few rickety plows, or drew small loads of firewood during the winter season.

Yet the place attracted Negroes, of the thriftless kind, like apple pomace attracts bees. Even the Negro preacher took up his residence here. Whether he recognized a field ripe for harvest of souls or whether he was moved by more mundane motives was known only to him and God. The Reverend MacGruder would speak in sanctified tone of his "mission" among his "brethren." Meanwhile he lived in a double log cabin with Sister Jinny Trotter, whose fast-growing brood of children, from the first three downward, recognized the Reverend as "pappy." Jinny herself made no secret of their paternity. She made no excuses, nor did the Reverend MacGruder. But Jinny did drop one illuminating statement by way of exculpation. She said: "Two clean sheets can't sile (soil) each other." She considered herself and the preacher as both notable religionists.

Captain Bob took his place and its riffraff inhabitants as largely a joke and said they were the happiest Negroes in the whole community. And indeed they were. He required some firewood at their hands and irregular portions of such produce as they made. His own wants were few, but these included irregular supplies of bad liquor he managed to come by in secret ways. Looking back I think it must have been that some of his more enterprising Negroes had for years a secret still up the river in a broken and wooded area that we called "The Bluffs." It was here to The Bluffs, so young tradition said, that the last panther retreated and made his home when the Big Woods to the east of the Little Duck began to fall before the encroaching need of new land for tobacco culture. Whether there was a panther in our area at this late period I do not know, but certainly this claim survived among the Negroes long after the Big Woods were gone. I myself, when about ten, heard an old Negro man claim his dog was killed by a "painter" while hunting possums near The Bluffs. I heard others say they had heard a "painter" cry in the night, "up de river, towards de Bluffs." I believed in the thing then, as Will and Edmund firmly did. But when I asked my father about it he laughed and said it was Negro talk, that there had been no panthers around in all his memory. I accepted this as fact, as I did all my father's statements; but while a boy I never wholly shook off the feeling that The Bluffs were somehow sinister.

Captain Bob Williams never spoke of the panther to me, nor did I to him. But somehow I got the idea, perhaps from the Negroes, that he encouraged the legend. Now, in retrospect after all these years, I think the thing unfolds—but only to convict me of prolonged childhood dumbness and credulity. Captain Bob's whiskey source must have lain in The Bluffs. I came to fish with him often before I was twelve years old. He, too, began to trap the river for mink and muskrat and beaver about that time. Beaver had returned in considerable numbers after years of absence from our river. This seems to have been due to gradual abandonment of cultivation of the bottom land, in turn due to summertime flooding, in turn again due to the slaughter of hillside timber.

Anyway, Captain Bob had a period of six or eight years in which he trapped the river. His trap line extended up and down the stream and he tended it in a flat-bottomed boat, which he mostly poled along the banks, where his traps were set. One Saturday afternoon in wintertime I was hunting our cows and came upon the Captain by the river putting out a trap where he showed me a muskrat "sign." He was always friendly toward me and on this occasion I manoeuvered an invitation to join him next morning on a visit to his traps. He appointed the time as ten o'clock at a sycamore tree near the river crossing. I was there, ahead of time, though I had left home for Sunday School. I waited long on the cold river bank, but the Captain ultimately arrived, coming down the river from toward The Bluffs. Already he had two beaver and ten muskrats in the bottom of the boat and was in high feather. He poled to the bank and I got in, counting his catch before I offered to pole. My offer he refused and handed me his one oar and said I might row. This I did with a will, because I was cold, because I felt the honor, and because of anticipation of the game we would take at the coming traps. I was not disappointed. Between the river crossing and the mouth of the Little Duck two miles below, and the end of the line, we took one otter, two more beaver, and seven additional muskrat. It was a memorable day! My only unease was that my mother would worry when I stayed away all day. For this I did, spending the whole afternoon with the Captain, pushing the boat back up the river to a point nearest his house. From here we lugged the catch in two trips. We even made a beginning with the skinning. We undressed the otter and one beaver before I left for home. I carried a quarter of the beaver wrapped in old papers and was instructed by the Captain to assure my mother it was better than beef and was to be cooked in the same way. It was both. He said he would call in two Negroes, Alex and Jim, to finish the skinning.

There was no rift in my liking for Captain Williams in my earliest years. He would visit at our house, especially in summer, and sit in the shade of our trees talking with my father. Father had a large tolerance for him despite his shiftless ways. Yet the Captain was not a good conversationalist. He read no books or papers or pretended to any learning. He seemed to look neither backward nor forward. He lived in the present. It was as if his fires had burnt out and he had no interest in rekindling them. He speculated not at all about the future, and an after-life concept was out of his orbit of interest. Childishly I envied him his unconcern about preachers, the church, and what they stood for. Particularly I envied his freedom from the fears our ministry so frequently played upon about the horrible future state of those who failed to obey their behests. Captain Bob had no defiant attitude toward the church or its ministry; rather it was a sort of unawareness that they existed. This disinterest also extended to secular affairs—county, state, and nation. I never heard him talk politics in any connection and I think he never voted at all. His qualities were so largely negative that what little respect was accorded him was based upon the pre-war condition and status of the family. But the Captain himself made no demands on that account. This itself perhaps indicates a key to the man's inner self. Feeling no sense of worth he made no poses of worth.

Yet I have heard my father and mother relate something of his pre-war story, particularly of the brilliancy of his marriage and the accompanying social stir it made. He had been a handsome and well-dressed youth, with manners wholly acceptable. He had loved horses and dogs and been quite a playboy in the countryside among the slaveowning families. He had won the hand of an exceedingly fair damsel on a neighboring plantation. She was his cousin, and sister to the then young Squire, John Banks Bradsher. Her parents had just died, leaving her mistress of a home at seventeen. The next year she married young Bob Williams, with the normal prospect of life as a gracious lady on a slave plantation. My father and my mother, both in their late teens and not yet married, attended the Williams' "infare," and I have heard my mother say that Sally Williams was the loveliest bride she ever knew. The infare, my father confirmed, was a brilliant county event. In the succeeding year a son was born, named John. The next succeeding year brought the disruption of the National Union and the formation of the Southern Confederacy. A local volunteer company was quickly formed and the young Robert Williams, in his early twenties, was elected its captain. His social position and his personal popularity seem to have accounted for the choice. He rode away with the young volunteers on the fastest horse in our side of the county.

Our Two Captains

What happened to his spirit, to the inner man, what his experiences were in the great struggle, I do not know. My father's after verdict was that Captain Robert was not naturally a leader of men, that he lacked any quality of steel. But my father was, at twenty, in the second company that marched away, and so never knew any of the details of Captain Robert's service or experience in the war. So it may well have been the end of Captain Robert's world, to which he came back, that accounted for the subsequent quality of his life. That end was cataclysmic, both personally and institutionally. Sally Williams was dead and the young child John was in the hands of relatives. The slaves were freemen and now scattered and demoralized. The tattered Captain refused to take up the burden and attempt reconstruction. He made no outward gestures of despair. But he let things go, as if they had no meaning, When the Ku Klux Klan formed all around him he took no interest. He was neither for nor against anything. When the Negroes, his former slaves, began to drift back under the spell of a homing instinct, he made no move to organize his place and set them to work. He sometimes spoke of them as his "crows" but quite without bitterness. Once, years later when I had come to fish with him on the river, I made bold to ask why he did not make his Negroes work for him. He shut my inquisitive mouth with a statement and a question of his own. Its purport was: "I do nothing for them, why should they do things for me?" I was not enough of a social and economic diagnostician to reply, and so let the matter drop as none of my business.

Drink grew on the Captain as the weary years passed by, but even this he did not make obtrusive. He visited no homes when he was in his cups, though sometimes people, both white and black, found him by a roadside at night in a drunken sleep. Then he would be taken home to his house on the hill and turned over to young Johnny—if that youth could be found. But Johnny himself, now in his twenties, was a far-ranging young man, with no yen for work or an orderly life. Johnny managed to keep a horse of a decent kind and, after a while, as told earlier, organized the pack of hounds he trained for fox hunting. In this he was aided by his uncle, Dr. John Bradsher, who also had sporting proclivities.

This "hunt" for a time gave a bit of color to our countryside, though it soon came near breaking on the rock of class interests. John wanted to clear out the many nondescript mongrels owned by the ragamuffin Negroes on the Williams place. This would eliminate the necessity of keeping his own dogs penned. He began this clearance with a shotgun and ran into solid opposition from the Negro owners. Appeal was made to the weak but kindly Captain Bob, who was said to have told his son he would shoot dog for dog if he pressed his purpose. So John re-penned his pack and struggled hard to keep it supplied with food. Old Cleveland was his leader, with the able young dog Blaine as first assistant. Cleveland learned a trick of the hunt that marked him as a strategist of considerable note and that saved him many a weary mile. While the run was a straight-a-way, as it was likely to be in the first hour or two, old Cleveland led the pack with a sparingly used high bell-like bay. Then when the quarry tired, came to a period of distress, and began to turn or circle, or run in arcs, old Cleveland would silently drop out of leadership leaving that role to Blaine, the black-and-tan who was ever at his heels. But this manoeuver did not mean that the wise old dog had relinquished the hunt. Rather it meant the end was drawing close. Cleveland now used an uncanny and almost unerring judgment as to the tricks of the fox, which way he would turn, which hill he would circle, which swale he would cut straight through. So it was usually when Cleveland's voice had died and Blaine's ringing staccato was heard leading the pack that young Johnny and his uncle rode like the wind to be in at the kill.

From ambush, or from a short swift run, the rested old general would have finished the business and be lying by, licking his chops when the hunt came up.

Once I rode with this pair, bareback on a mule named Beck, and felt myself highly honored to be of the company. I fancied it was the beginning of a sporting career. Alas, it never turned out that way. Johnny soon went off to a restless clerkship in town. Captain Robert urged the dogs upon Dr. John Banks Bradsher, the other half-owner. The Doctor soon turned them out to shift for themselves. Old Cleveland returned, with Blaine at his heels, to the Williams place. There the Negroes drew them into rabbit hunts with their mongrels. With these I sometimes joined, and my interest was always in watching Cleveland and Blaine. The latter from the first would lead the mongrels after a freshly sprung hare. Not so old Cleveland. He wouldn't even start in the chase and never gave tongue at all for this small game. It was as if he had lost his voice outright. But he was still the strategist, still used his judgment as to which way the homing bunny would turn. He would take the short cuts and through the day he would kill more game than all the rest together. He was the only dog I personally ever knew who perfected this art.

Captain Robert, with his son gone, drank more and more and fished less and less. I saw him much less frequently, but he retained my interest and liking. Yet events were soon in the making that destroyed my regard. This came about over the widely publicized affair of the Captain's charging Wiley Buck, a strange, solitary Negro of the community, with arson and his prosecution in the courts. My father had defended this hapless Negro, and I had been wholly loyal in the belief of his innocence. But the issue and the outcome had estranged the Captain from our family and the difference was never thereafter bridged.

Though I judged him then, and judge him now, to have been a man without vindictiveness or hate, I have wondered at the turn of his mind toward my father after Wiley Buck was acquitted. He never spoke to him again. To me he would only grunt if we met in the road and I rendered my accustomed greeting. Explanation doubtless lies in his firm conviction that the Negro was guilty and that the act came so near to destroying the old Williams house, the place where all his memories dwelt, where he had been born, where he had been a hopeful boy with his parents in a place of luxury, where for a few short years he had had his beautiful wife, Miss Sally.

Probably a vision of its burning was evoked in his mind and deeply printed there when the near-by quarters of Ellen, his Negro cook, whom Wiley Buck was said to have molested, were destroyed by the fire which he was convinced Wiley Buck had set. What mattered the fate of a dim-wit Negro? His shrine had been at stake, the only shrine he had ever had. It held all the man had ever held dear. Doubtless its loss would have meant the final toppling of his world, or that one little corner he cared about.

Hence, looking back a long time after, I think perhaps I gather the one main reason for Captain Robert's vindictive prosecution of the Negro Wiley Buck as accused arsonist. It was hate; for the Captain on the stand at the Negro's trial had boldly stated in the face of judge and jury that he now wished he had shot "the devil" when he drove him from the place following his encounter with Ellen.

So all my old liking for the Captain had turned into a reluctant aversion. I had grown into my late teens before the Captain died. His end came suddenly, when he was all alone at night in the once fine old house on the hill. Informed by a Negro messenger, John came out from the town and had his father buried in the old walled family plot up the ridge from the house. No religious office was performed, which was fitting. A few relatives gathered along with a host of Negroes from his own and neighboring places. For the latter it was a distinctive holiday, setting itself apart from the well-nigh perpetual holidays of the Williams Negroes. I sensed that my father would have attended the burial except for its unfitness in view of Captain Robert's last years of enmity.

The facts of the Captain's end soon softened my latter feeling toward him and awakened my earlier memories of shared experiences. Also Wiley Buck's tragic end was just a few years past. Both were now beyond anybody's harm. Or were they? I turned this thought over in my mind, and from side to side. I had come up where nothing was so firmly fixed as that when you died you were "saved" or "damned." The only wee doubt in my mind that this was natural law lay in the fact that I had never heard my father say so. All the preachers confirmed the fact and all the people round about seemed to acquiesce. All save a few like Captain Robert Williams and Captain Robert Sergeant, who took no interest in the matter at all. And I wondered if my father did, though I knew his life was quite unlike theirs. He went to church in a regular way, even led many a useful community enterprise. But he never grew emotional in church, as many another did. Nor had I ever heard him say a prompting "Amen" when the preacher was separating the sheep from the goats and driving the latter into the pit. I had often wondered where he stood in the premises but I had feared to ask lest he might confirm what I did not like to believe.

So the matter had rested until Captain Robert's passing. Then the question resurrected itself. But I had no great trouble in settling the matter. Maybe increasing age was some help. Anyway, I stood so straight I leaned backward in the Captain's favor. Also I may have been helped in saving Captain Robert from the fires of the burning pit by a fortuitous contact with an old, old Negro man, "Uncle Jenk," on the Williams place soon after the Captain died. I fell into talk with him one day as he sat weaving a rough oak-split basket. I asked if he missed seeing Captain Bob around. Yes, he missed seeing him about. "Yo see, I knowed him all his life. I knowed his pappy, Marse Will, do' he died when I was young." The old Negro was silent a bit, smoothing a split with his knife. I feared he would not resume, that his mind would run off into dreams of his own childhood. Then he spoke again: "I minds Cap'n Bob when he wus a little bitty boy, pulling at Miss Jonsie's knee. Miss Jonsie wus my old Miss. She was good to all us chillun, and made us clo's." In his own good time, and in his own way, old Uncle Jenk gave me much of biography of the Williams family—much of which I had heard from my parents. Finally I manoeuvered him around to the point of the particular question in my mind. I wanted his opinion as to the future state of one like Captain Robert. I didn't ask him outright, but he got the point of my interest. "Suttinly," he said, "dar oughta be a place, not too hot, fer fokes lak Cap'n Bob ter go." Pause, then: "Fer Cap'n sholy laked de shade."

This conversation with old Uncle Jenk reinforced my conviction as to Captain Robert's deserts. So I consigned him to an intermediate place, not too warm and not too cool, a place where the sun shone all day until the shadows grew long down under the hills along the fishing stretches of the river. Here for me the Captain has lived all these years, perhaps journeying now and then up as far as The Bluffs where the "painter" used to scream and now is long since silent. I would not like to go again to that place, a place I never thoroughly explored, though it was comparatively close by. I suppose the great trees are all gone, the rocks of the long cliff exposed to the blaze of the sun, and the river below all choked with silt and debris. Much rather would I keep the picture, now long in my mind, of heavy dark forest, and clear crystal water flowing over the ledge below the cliff, where the "painter" comes to drink, where, in a little secret nook tucked away under a ledge and the overhanging trees, is a little copper "still," with a little crooked old black man tending the little furnace that boils the mash. Here comes the shade of Captain Robert Williams, in his worn-out shoes and his battered old hat, with a fishing rod in his dirty hands and a sigh of relief from his gruelling walk. It is there I have preferred to leave him all these years and for me there he shall remain. What matter if he were a sinner? What matter if he never conformed? What matter what the "good people" say? He could not bring back an order that was gone; nor did they!

The Revival

Through the years, I look back upon the institutions and customs of the countryside where I was born and where I had my early life. I have never been so far removed from it that my interest has faded. Yet I have gathered perspective as the years have passed by. I have come to appraise some of our customs in a truer way than when I shared so intimately in them. There was the "revival," for instance, a characteristic and important feature of rural community life wherever the Methodists or the Baptists were strong.

In my community, overwhelmingly Methodist, the week of the revival was a peak of the year. It was staged in mid-summer by the circuit rider in agreement with the elders of the church when the crops had been well worked out and the harvest period not yet begun. It was a season of physical relaxation, of spiritual renewal, of social contacts and refreshment. Every day there was dinner in the grove of trees on the church grounds.

All looked forward to this week. It was almost as much a peak of the year in our community as was Christmastime. Apart from the serious business of religion, when the tide was at its flood in a successful revival, the elders talked crops and matters of general interest. The women worked over the dinners and minded their babies and kept the very young in order. To the young generation the period was a continuous feast of exciting contacts.

The word "revival" and the institution it covered in Southern Methodism needs no definition to the Methodists of the past century. In the present era the institution has well-nigh passed out, even in the rural districts of this church. Its theory was that the communicants in the church, that is, the officially inducted membership, needed periodically a re-stimulation of their religious zeal, a re-vivification of their faith, a re-affirmation of their vows of loyalty—in short, a spiritual boost. This concept and the use of the revival included two other accepted ideas of the period: one, the restoration to the arms of the church of all members who had undergone the process known as "backsliding" (or "falling from grace"); and two, the addition to membership of all whom the revival services "converted." The backslider, a definitely recognized element in the church, was a person who had at some former time been converted, had become a member by taking the vows of the church, and had afterward grown lukewarm, negligent, or wholly indifferent to the binding obligation of those vows. Stated somewhat more specifically, the backslider was a person who had reverted, both in his own conception and in the eyes of the community, to the classification of "sinner." He had fallen from grace. In effect, the point that distinguished a backslider from a regular sinner was that the former had neither been dismissed from the church membership nor had formally withdrawn his name. He was a reproach to the membership but was a straying sheep who must be kindly dealt with and recovered to the fold.

This work of re-folding straying sheep was as much the task of a revival as was the work of bringing into the fold the lost sheep, sinners, who had never been inside. The technique was not essentially different—conversion for the sinner of the latter class, re-conversion for the backslider. Yet the backslider might avail himself of simple re-affirmation of faith strengthened by renewal of vows. In other words, he might resume where he had left off; while the plain sinner must run the whole course of conversion and induction. The great majority of the sinner class, as distinguished from backsliders, was the up-coming generation, children and young people, the regular reservoir of recruitments to keep up and increase the membership. Among them, of course, was an occasional "hardened" sinner, a person who had reached adulthood, or even passed into declining years, without ever having yielded to social pressure and been converted. Such an individual might be a good and right-living person, or he might be a rank reprobate. Yet in either case he was a lost sheep unless and until he was enfolded in the arms of the church.

All this important work of the revival rested more heavily upon the circuit rider (preacher), who served the particular church, than upon any other. This was one of his main responsibilities. Some were especially fitted for the task and looked forward to the revival period when their special gifts as spiritual leaders might be brought into play. Such special gifts varied, as did the technique of their employment, but a primary one was the "gift of tongues"—an ease of speech, coupled with a close familiarity with the Scriptures. Imagination, logic, a fundamentalist faith, and a fervid zeal were other ingredients that made up the equipment of a successful revivalist. Many a Methodist preacher of that era had these qualities in high degree and could and did make his revival services the peak of his whole year's work. In such instances the local community was profoundly stirred; an emotional tension would grip the whole body of the membership and its waves extend outward to engulf the unredeemed.

An additional quality of the successful revivalist was his ability to wake the zeal, and therefore the aid, of the staunchest element of the church's membership—both men and women. This zeal and this aid were automatically held by many a member as automatically due, a part of their personal obligation to assist in saving souls. And I am sure it went even deeper, and tied up with the inherent tendency in human nature to set his neighbor straight in matters that concerned eternal salvation. So, in the church in every local community there were always to be found a zealous few who could be utterly depended upon by the preacher as his shock troops in a revival service. The way and manner of the exercise of this aid varied with the individual and with his or her predilections, special gifts, and standing in the community. Yet the role had evidently been evolutionary and, in the period here concerned, consisted in the main of some half-dozen different forms of endeavor.

First was the art of public prayer. In practically every Methodist church community there was to be found one or more men among the membership who was naturally gifted in this art, or had cultivated it from modest first attempts to a point where real eloquence, whipped up by religious zeal and profound emotional impulse, was not the infrequent result. Doubly effective was such a man whose piety and day-to-day religious life were things known to the community at large. Such a man commanded respect of his hearers when he talked to the Lord. Even fascination gripped many, and hearty "amens," and even sobs, were often wrested from the more emotional. The preacher, if he was a good psychologist—and he often was—knew just the moment in a revival to employ this powerful aid, an aid the more effective because it rarely bore the least taint of insincerity. Often, therefore, such prayers and their "offerers" were as effective as the logic, the imagery, or the fervid oratory of the preacher himself, and sometimes more so. Backsliders were reclaimed and sinners were converted under the powerful stimulus of such prayers offered in the simple faith that God heard the earnest appeal of his servant and directly intervened to turn the erring soul into the way of righteousness.

A second type of assistance to the end of making a revival truly successful was that furnished by especially zealous members who, when the moment was ripe (a period when emotional fervor had been got well under way by the sermon, the appeal of the preacher, and the prayer which followed), passed about in the congregation and talked to sinners and backsliders. This role was usually taken by women, which it seemed to embarrass less. This appeal to the individual was necessarily made in an undertone in order to keep the whole proceeding orderly. The object was to induce the sinner to take the "first step," which consisted in the routine of arising, going to the altar of the church, and there kneeling in penitence and asking forgiveness of God for his sins. At the altar attended other specialists who took over the task of guiding the penitent through the miracle process of conversion. This consisted in an arrival at the conviction that one's sins had been forgiven, the soul made clean and now acceptable to God. This point, arrived at under the full tide of emotional waves beating upon the "seeker," and surcharging the whole group, was the climax for the individual, who arose and proclaimed that he was born anew.

Nor can it be questioned that this was often true. I have in memory numerous instances in which this experience was a turning point in the moral life of particular individuals. Others, of course, were not long or profoundly affected. The process, despite all its embarrassments, brought most of the young people into the church and some older ones who had escaped, including backsliders. Some, of course, escaped again when the emotional upheaval had worn off, a few in fact becoming perennial backsliders—to the half-scandal of the staunchest portion of the truly Christian part of the membership. Nevertheless this small group furnished continuing grist for the millstones of the revival until the mood and the concepts upon which the practice was founded had themselves in time worn away in face of a rising sophistication.

Congregational singing of inspirational and devotional hymns was another and very powerful method of sustaining a revival and rolling up the emotional momentum that made its objectives attainable. Psychologists have long understood the power of music to float the soul of the individual out of the orbit of self and unite the spirit of man in a common whole. Organized religion in all ages and in all stages of human evolution has used it to this end. Without it the majesty of the Christian church, of whatever division or creed, could never have been half so imposing. Hence it is no strange thing that congregational singing was a most intimate and effective part of Methodist revivals and that in this church, as in all others, it is so fundamental a part of worship that it must of necessity outlast all other practices.

In Methodist revivals of the past century the hymns for congregational singing were chosen with an eye to the particular stage of procedure, yet without any rigid adherence to that procedure. Improvisation, to meet a particular situation that might have arisen, was always possible. A song that would bite deep into the emotions at a critical stage, would raise the victory cry against the cohorts of evil; a song that would speak peace to a troubled and weary soul; one that would awaken memory of a departed loved one—the whole gamut of songs whose words and music drew away the self-consciousness of the individual and impelled him to conform to the religious formula required for a righteous life. Many of our hymns were written by Charles Wesley, in the period of the rise of Methodism under the nurture and fervid zeal of John Wesley, the great organizer, founder and inspirer of the Methodist movement in eighteenth-century England. Conceding the power of music and lyrical poetry directed to an inspirational end, Charles Wesley must always have high place in any appraisal of the profound effects of Methodism upon religious history of the past two centuries.

The picture of the Methodist practice of the revival would be incomplete were it not pointed out that the institution was not static in any period of its history. It, like most institutions, religious or secular, was subject to the law of growth and change. It had reached its climax around the end of the nineteenth century and begun a slow decline. For instance, as has been pointed out, it was the long-time obligation of the circuit rider (preacher), and even clergyman in charge of a station (one church in a town) to hold an annual revival at each of his churches. This entailed a very heavy burden upon the preacher in charge of a circuit of from three to five churches. The wells of spiritual zeal were likely to run dry, even in the case of the most gifted preachers. All the revivals were staged in the summertime, a period most suited to the convenience of a rural community. Hence this was, for the preacher, by far the heaviest period of his year's work. And yet it must be performed, in the earlier period, largely by himself in the central role, assisted by the spiritually-minded laymen (and lay women) in the individual church. It must also be observed that not every preacher in charge of a circuit, or even of a station, possessed the gift of tongues, the dynamic spiritual drive, and the psychological qualifications that were requisite for a successful revival.

The Revival

Hence the practice grew up of the preacher-in-charge securing the help of another preacher in the conference connection to aid him in his week of revival at his individual churches. Such individuals were available mainly from the stations whose preacher had charge of only one church and, therefore, was obligated for only one revival of his own. Thus his summer was largely free as contrasted with that of the preacher in charge of a circuit. Of course not every preacher in charge of a station was indubitably qualified with the gifts of a successful revivalist. But many of them were. They had, oftener than not, attained the charge of a station by virtue of superior qualifications in education, zeal, and general equipment for leadership.

The stations, all in the towns, were the better-paid posts in the church, the church there generally being composed of a wealthier membership than that of a rural church. Hence such a church could readily support the cost of a full-time minister, while the rural churches must be grouped into circuit units and divide the time of the preacher assigned to the circuit. Therefore the station preacher was likely to be the better prepared, the better paid, and the better provided with that leisure that was necessary for quiet study to further increase his effectiveness. A natural consequence was that the ablest of such station preachers were much in demand by the circuit riders who needed assistance in holding summertime revivals. This assistance, oftentimes the actual leadership of the revival, was ordinarily furnished without expectation or offer of material reward. It was a labor of love, prompted by zeal for the cause of the church in saving souls. If, incidentally, it enhanced the reputation by advertising the spiritual power of the preacher, then that was a matter in conformity with the general law of life governing successful careers in one's chosen work.

In the end, however, the trail blazed by the abler and more zealous station preachers in assisting or assuming charge of revivals for less well-equipped or overworked preachers, led to the rise of the professional evangelists. Indeed this type of preacher had been gradually emerging through much of the nineteenth century and was at the peak of influence in its last twenty years. Most church denominations in America experienced the influence of the evangelists, who were but a sublimated species of the revivalist. Of the greater denominations of Protestantism perhaps the Baptists and the Methodists (in that order) produced the greatest impulse toward Evangelism in the nineteenth century, this becoming a strong echo of the great Congregationalist movement of the eighteenth century crowned by the work of Jonathan Edwards in New England. Spurgeon was pre-eminent, and had no peer in the Baptist group; while Dwight L. Moody was pre-eminent among Methodists. Both had superlative powers in moving great masses of men. Both had many lesser imitators, some with scarcely less power and skill. Among the Methodists perhaps Sam Jones and Billy Sunday, after Moody, were the greatest exponents of the movement, possessing more of natural eloquence and knowledge of herd psychology than any of the hosts of other preachers attracted to this field. And their imitators scaled all the way down to cheap and insincere persons capitalizing upon the opportunity that the prevailing mood of religion presented.

But it is not here intended to dig into the history of the wide-sweeping revivalist movement in America, but rather to present the simple procedures of the Methodist Church that were common to all its individual units and particularly to the rural church community in the late nineteenth century. It was in these units, basic in the whole church edifice, that the ground was unconsciously prepared for the all-embracing Methodist Revival on a nation-wide scale.

So, back in the simple Methodist revival in the average rural church, as in the station churches in the town, the spirit of commercialism crept in naturally when some preachers who formerly assisted, without pay, the overburdened circuit rider in holding his annual revival, had made reputation enough, gained confidence enough, to pass into the ranks of the minor evangelists. They began to expect pay for their assistance and, at the same time, their prestige enabled them to assume chief direction of the revival, the regular preacher dropping into

The Revival

the role of assistant to the professional. The remuneration to the revivalist was necessarily on the contingent basis, dependent upon the depth to which the community was stirred in the revival and the sum total of the voluntary contributions the community would make when, at the climax of soul-stirring, the touch was made.

This part of the business was tactfully left to the regular minister, with something of a behind-the-scene understanding between him and the revivalist in respect to the propitious moment. Also the regular preacher had normally felt out for the influence as well as the aid of the chief or important members of the church—usually those who were best able to pay. These preliminary understandings arranged, the local preacher, at the strategic moment—always just before the announced close of the revival and when the emotional tension was at its height—would take charge of proceedings and make the appeal for contributions. He pointed out that the Spirit of God had been in their midst, that there had been a great harvest of souls for the Kingdom, that God had used his agent (the visiting revivalist) as an instrument to this end and that a laborer was worthy of his hire. Of course the laborer himself was present, seated behind the altar, looking benign and exhausted.

The art of taking the contribution had many nuances and varying techniques. Sometimes the method was to call for individual initiative from the congregation. In such case the most materially solid members were expected to rise and mention the amount of their gifts. From these varying but largest amounts to be expected, the less materially solid members ran down the scale to the smallest voluntary contribution. The sum total, paid in cash at the end of the service, constituted the pay to the visiting revivalist. Sometimes the preacher in charge, out of fear that a wholly voluntary first subscription of an able member might be too low, himself mentioned a beginning sum. "Who had been so blessed, and seen his loved ones, his friends, and neighbors so blessed" that he would give two hundred dollars to the cause of God? From such a sum the standard would be constantly lowered and fitted in with each individual's willingness and capacity to pay. Here, of course, two forces were now working: one, the exaltation of the emotional mood, not yet subsided; and, two, caution and practicability attendant upon gifts of money. Indeed it is not too much to say that at this stage in Methodist revivals in a rural church a hot and cold current came into sudden collision, with the consequent result of lowering the spiritual temperature, though certainly not immediately to the point of the pre-revival period.

There was always a residuum of effect lasting for longer or shorter periods. Some had actually been set on a new course in life; some had been brought to an awakening of thought processes; some had made new vows or new resolutions. Some walked more humbly before God out of sheer regard for consistency with protestations made in public. Some, of course, shed their recent exaltation within a month, or even a shorter time. A thoughtful few remained befogged mentally and spiritually, asking themselves what it was all about, how much of it was real and how much unreal. To the wholly thoughtless it had been an emotional "jag," the implications of which they understood not at all.

But along with these very mixed spiritual results there were other social results, possibly less obvious, or tangible, yet possessing their value in the community life as a whole. These were products of the physical relaxation, the social contacts of men, of women, of young people and children, before and after church, and especially at the noon hour around the dinner tables in the shadows of the trees. The food was always well-prepared and good, each housewife vying with others in the excellence of her basket or box of the best things the countryside afforded. There were always large platters of finely cured country ham, of young fried chicken, brown and crisp, of many cakes of different varieties—baked in deep round molds, or in inch loaves to be piled one on top of another up to six or eight, to be cut all the way through in wedge-shaped sections and taken off by the feasters in such thickness as appetite dictated.

And there were gargantuan appetites around most of the

The Revival

tables. Most of the men of our community worked hard on the land, either in its management or in its actual cultivation. All led outdoor lives all the year round. Also, there were ordinarily not a few visitors from adjacent church communities, perhaps on the same circuit, and having relatives, friends, and acquaintances in our community. These were likely to come in the latter half of the week of revival, when the information had spread that a "real revival spirit" was present, that the preaching was good and the community profoundly stirred. Sometimes visitors came from the nearest village or town, the pious impelled by spiritual impulse, others by the opportunity for contacts and good food. Of this latter class of visitors, usually young people of both sexes, one unconsciously gathered a mixed impression of the effect of their presence. Our own young people, boys and girls alike, found pleasure in the visitors, deriving stimulation from the opposite sex in each group. This was normal, for there was no wide gulf of a social sort between the best of our community and the best of the town. Perhaps a hardly perceptible difference in manners and dress, and a shade of difference in effects of the sun upon outdoor skins and indoor skins, was all that set the groups apart—and youth took scant cognizance of these. Besides, there was much of blood relationship between the town dweller and the rural dweller, and this formed a solid basis for their intermingling.

Yet one other facet of this contact of the townspeople of the younger generation with the rural church in its revival week must needs be noted to make the picture truthful. This aspect was less perceived than merely felt. It consisted of a rising sentiment, mainly among the religious elders of the country community, that the young people of the town were less inclined to religious influence than the youth of the country; that their influence upon the latter was a thing to be suspected and watched to the end that it wrought no evil. The circuit preacher, and sometimes the visiting preacher or the revivalist, undoubtedly shared, or even gave shape to this sentiment. These latter tended to regard the young of the town as more sophisticated, and less amenable to the current of emotions they were seeking to effect. In short, the implication was that the youth of the town were likely to impede the work of the spirit. Looking back upon the era of the country revival as I witnessed it, I now have the conviction that this attitude was rather strong, but that it mainly affected the religious leaders rather than the community as a whole. Certainly this was true of my own rural community—for it was healthful-minded enough in a social way to be unconsciously confident that it could absorb all comers.

One other feature of a rural community revival lingers in my mind as part of the picture that is now so rapidly fading from the memory of men. This feature concerns the changes of numerous sorts, wrought in the life of the countryside by the arrival of the motor car. The rural revival as partially pictured above, is a scene out of the horseback and horse-and-buggy age. Its characteristic features began a transition all but simultaneously with the development of motor transportation, thus leading to the question whether the quickened tempo of life was the main factor that undermined the fundamentalist attitude in religion upon which the Methodist revival was so largely predicated. Whatever the answer to that question it probably would not, could not, represent the whole truth. But it is a well-recognized social fact that the last-century rural revival as well as the great city revival, with its high-powered evangelist and all the paraphernalia of music leaders and choir singers, has in this century passed into a decline that points toward early complete disappearance.

So the picture of the institution at its peak will be but a record of a past phase of social history, and that history would not be nearly complete unless the physical setting was painted in.

The average North Carolina rural church, of the Methodists as well as the other denominations, was usually set in a grove of trees, the grounds usually being well-chosen and containing several acres. The site had sometimes been bought by the group of persons who desired to form a congregation, erect a house for worship, and maintain it as a community center. Not infrequently the site was donated by a leader in the movement.

Normally it was large enough to provide space for a burial ground. This burial ground was laid off into plots assigned originally to individual heads of families. Space was left for later assignments when the need arose.

Here in these plots the elders lay first, by process of nature, men and their wives and children who died young. Sons who married and had families of their own were likely to acquire a separate plot from the unassigned area, and thus the community of the dead was constantly increased as the years passed by. In the earlier days the burial ground (later called the cemetery) was undifferentiated from the church grounds by fence or wall and for long was not very well kept. Later, with improving economic conditions, came greater attention to the burial ground. Fences, usually of "palings" painted white, and later walls of stone came to mark out the area. Simultaneously came the use of marble slabs (and rarely a monument shaft) to replace the crude stones set up at head and foot to mark the resting place of each of the dead. On these slabs were carved the name, dates of birth and death, and a pious inscription, sometimes a favorite verse from the Scriptures, sometimes a couplet from a favorite and familiar hymn. Here the dead rested, the memory of them gradually fading out as the generations came and went. The memory of a man, or woman, who had been especially marked in the community, or had gone out from it and made a career, of course lingered longest by virtue of natural community pride. A beautiful community custom nearly always existed of bringing flowers to church on preaching days and placing them on graves of departed relatives. This, however, was individual rather than general application, depending upon the depth of memory and affection left in the hearts of those who yet survived.

The architecture of the rural Methodist church has undergone a rather slow evolution from quite crude to very much more tasteful and adequate buildings. This of course is the product of economic changes reflecting themselves in increasing taste and greater pride. Better built houses for worship, painted, and with current for lighting and a furnace for heat, seem normal to the present generation. The cruder houses of the past century are but a fading memory. None except the very oldest in my home community remember when the interior of our church had a built-in panel down the longest axis, from the altar to the door, which divided the seating according to sex. This was in keeping with the old custom formulated in the early days of Methodism in the eighteenth century. Many other Protestant sects, especially those tinged with the spirit of John Calvin, followed the same custom. In my earliest memory of my own community church, this custom was beginning to break down, though it yet required something of a bold spirit for a young man and a young woman to march in and sit together on the same side of the panel. Curiously, it was the young man who had to take the initiative in the breach of this custom and brazen it out on the woman's side of the church. Perhaps that was natural—for thereby he offered proof to the young woman that he would dare all things for her favor.

The generous size of the grove and church grounds area was, in horse-and-buggy days, doubtless as much dictated by the need of room for vehicles and horses as by the cheapness of land. There, especially in revival periods, when attendance was apt to be large, horses and mules were detached from the vehicles and tied to limbs and trees furthest back from the church. Many of them, though not all, were fed by their owners during the dinner hour.

At our church it was customary to make sure that no visitor or other person, well-to-do or poor, who had not brought provision, should fail to get an invitation to some table. These tables in my earliest memory were individual family tables, and members of the family invited whom they would to eat with them. The individual tables were well scattered over the grove under the shade of the trees. Sometimes several families, usually relatives, combined their food at a common table. This led to a larger crowd and greater sociability. Later the custom came to be to place all the tables together in a long row and the preacher, before the recess hour, delivered a general invitation for all present to partake of the generous and excellent food the women of the church always provided.

Being but a boy when these scenes of the past fixed themselves in my memory, I think I might be held guiltless of levity if I point out that dogs in our community seemed greatly to enjoy the revival season. They came in generous numbers, dogs of all descriptions, following their owners' wagons, carriages, or buggies—with well-stuffed food baskets or boxes inside. These dogs had a social season of contacts, but the peak of their day was the dinner hour when they passed about among the feasters around the tables and received the wealth of bones and broken food thrown down by their human friends. Sometimes two dogs, desirous of the same bit, would come to clash, much to the interest of small boys in the group. But usually they were peaceful and courteous, proceeding on the assumption that where there was so much there would be plenty for all. And truly there was! For I have seen dogs at revivals with sides so distended that they would pass over a discarded chunk of delicious cake with a disdainful sniff. I knew one dog who, I had reason to believe, remained on the church grounds at night throughout revival week, not giving himself the trouble of journeying home and back again. Perhaps he was chagrined when a day came and the crowd did not return. But even so, he had already well-lined ribs and the memory of glorious feasting.

Now and again some pet dog with a strong attachment for his master or mistress, or to a child, would slip through an open door of the church seeking out the object of his affections. His presence, thrust in upon the services, was likely to create a diversion, especially among the young fry, to the disgruntlement of the preacher. How could the spirit flow when attention was diverted by the uncertain actions of a puzzled dog? The picture here called up brings to mind a story told in my father's house by the Rev. G. W. Ivey. Mr. Ivey at that time was in charge of the Leasburg Circuit of which our church, Concord, was a part. His was a strong and interesting personality, commanding respect and affection both as spiritual leader and man. For long years he was one of the most effective circuit riders in our denomination, serving charges from the mountains to the sea. On the occasion to which I refer he was conducting a revival at Concord church. Returned in the late afternoon from the arduous services at church, he and my father were sitting in chairs drawn out on the lawn to catch the breezes. I sat on the grass and listened—for I knew him to be an interesting teller of stories. The talk turned to dogs in church, of which there had been an instance that very day.

Mr. Ivey said: "Once, when I was holding a revival on the Lenoir circuit, up in the mountains, the services were held in a shady brush arbor built for the purpose. Dogs were pretty thick, but generally well-behaved. But one afternoon, during my closing prayer, a little fice dog strayed in up near the altar. He became excited at my voice and began to yap in competition. I suppose I *was* pretty fervid. As I continued my prayer the little dog drew closer and closer, raising such a clamor that it was quite confusing. Finally he was in reach of my hand. I reached out quickly and seized him by the neck. I went on with my prayer, forgetting the little dog. When I had finished, and withdrew my hand, the poor little fellow was dead!"

Uncle Calvin and His Five Sons

Uncle Calvin was born a slave. At what date I do not know, nor did he. The Sergeant family, who owned his parents as well as himself and his wife, did not keep accurate plantation records, or else they were not preserved. He lived on our place, formerly called a "plantation," from the end of the Civil War to the early nineties. This plantation was in the old tobacco section which in very early times had extended down into Carolina from Virginia as that crop spread. It was cut by the South Hyco which, with its twin the North Hyco, made up the Hycotee. The Hycotee entered the Dan. The Dan joined with the Staunton and flowed into the broad Roanoke, and this into Albemarle Sound.

Here I was born at the end of "Reconstruction times," a misnomer—for reconstruction, social and economic, was hardly begun.

Living in the present, as small boys do, I had little thought for the wrecking past. But I knew the fields and streams and woods and what was in them. My playmates were black children of the soil and this seemed quite natural to them and me. I respected my elders, both white and black. I called old Negroes "Uncle" and "Aunt" without any sense of artificiality. My white elders, too, were "Uncle," or "Aunt," or "Cousin"—whether blood kin or not. I worked in the fields—as my ancestors had not done. I worshipped my father, who had a large tolerance, but whose will was law. Our acres were broad, but rarely smiling with fatness. My father operated them mainly by the use of wage "hands" (Negroes hired for a monthly wage and keep). Sharecropping, however, was a competing system. This system involved letting land to a cropper and "furnishing" him with living quarters, a team (horses or mules) and necessary equipment. Food for the team fell to the landlord's charge, as did also five-eighths of the cost of fertilizer (necessary particularly for tobacco and used sparingly for other products). Division of the crops, or their sales price, was five-eighths to the landlord and three-eighths to the cropper. The cropper, not versed in fractions, called the system "farming for half after the fourth," this based on the right of one-fourth to the landlord for use of the land and half of the remainder for his other costs. Under this system the landlord kept an oversight of the cropper's main operations, particularly if the cropper were lacking in energy, skill, or dependability.

Uncle Calvin moved to our place as a sharecropper, having shifted there from the neighboring Sergeant place at the end of the Civil War. I am sure he was my father's first experiment with this now much abused system. Uncle Calvin's move was apparently made largely for the purpose of demonstrating that he was now a free man and could do as he pleased. He and his wife, Aunt Harriet, continued to hold the Sergeants, Uncle John and Cousin Delphia, in respect and affection. About once a month, on a Sunday, they went to see them and stayed for dinner in the kitchen.

On our place the pair and their family had been assigned a double log cabin, with a large squat chimney of well-chosen stones running up between the two rooms. A wide fireplace was in each room. The roof, of heart-pine shingles, was continuous over both rooms and the two recesses, one on either side of the broad chimney. One of these recesses, that on the back side of the house, boarded up and with a small door, was used for storage space. The other recess was a passageway by the chimney between doors in each room. Beside, on the front, was a door to each room, placed in the middle.

The house was of enduring oak logs, built before the middle of the century, and formed part of a quadrangle of cabins down back of our house in the grove above. Slaves had occupied these houses before the Civil War. Afterward "wage hands" and croppers took their places, being for the most part the same personnel. When my memory first awakened, some of these quarters for the Negroes on the place had disappeared.

Uncle Calvin and His Five Sons

But the one in which Uncle Calvin and Aunt Harriet lived was long enduring, so stoutly was it built. Perhaps the character and qualities of its occupants also had something to do with its preservation. Uncle Calvin would be insistent for repairs if his roof sprung a leak, or a plank was worn out in the floor.

Aunt Harriet was a careful and tidy soul and kept a neat house—that is, the room in which she and Uncle Calvin lived. The other room, where the five boys lived, was a more difficult matter. She described this room as "higgy-piggy" and constantly berated her sons for their slovenly ways. She even called upon Uncle Calvin to back up her protestations with a stout switch. This method of discipline was applied only to the youngest two—little Daniel and Edmund. With Dave it could have wrought no change.

There were five sons, and no daughters, born to the couple. In order they were Raphael (Rafe), Joseph (Joe), David (Dave), Little Daniel, and Edmund. The first three were grown men when I first remember them. Uncle Calvin called his group of workers his "force" and, loosely, the term included himself, though not Aunt Harriet. He and his force required two mules and Uncle Calvin was careful that these be of the best, not broken-down or outworn stock. These mules he thought of as almost his own, and he and his sons gave them careful treatment. They were always the sleekest animals on the place, barring, perhaps, a riding horse for my father.

All Uncle Calvin's sons were different in characteristics and quality. The eldest, Rafe, was a Lothario to the young Negro women of our place and those adjoining. To his father he was a beloved Absalom. Aunt Harriet, who was religious, had striven mightily to rear all her children in the fear and admonition of the Lord. Uncle Calvin had depended upon his gospel of work as the saving grace. But Rafe, usually biddable about the work, went his own way in affairs of the heart. The inevitable happened.

Ella, a light-brown girl of eighteen years, came from the Sergeants to bring a sad story to Rafe's father and mother. She was "six months gone," she said, with Rafe's child, and was minded to "swear it" to him unless matrimony took place, as he had promised. Rafe denied the promise and proved stubborn about putting his neck in the yoke.

Uncle Calvin, advised by my father, went across the Hyco to consult Squire Grandy Winstead, who had much experience in handling such matters. "Swearing to" the paternity of children under the then "maintenance law" left much discretion to justices of the peace in settling such issues. Squire Grandy was known to be fair and just. So Uncle Calvin went to consult. He himself was quite befuddled about what was to be done. He dreaded to see his best-loved son coerced. He half believed that Ella was a designing hussy, that her tale might not be true. He had observed her often at the Sergeants and had noted the carefree way she swung her hips. He insisted to Aunt Harriet that Ella was a "sassy gal" and that her mammy was a "wench."

But the law was the law, and white men said it must be enforced. When he returned from his interview with Squire Grandy, Aunt Harriet questioned him about results. "He say," reported Uncle Calvin, "Rafe, he stood up in de sweet, now he mus' stan' up in de bitter." Even so, he connived at Rafe's avoidance of matrimony and agreed to be bound with his son for one hundred and twenty-five dollars (borrowed from my father), that the Squire assessed against the stubborn defendant.

This penalty, not an infrequent one under the law of the period, was supposed to serve several purposes. One, to curb young men like Rafe; two, salve the wounded virtue of young women like Ella; and, three, to protect the common good. The burden in the main fell upon Uncle Calvin and Aunt Harriet. The penalty was heavy for the resources of the debtors. Maybe some of the burden did drift to Rafe in Uncle Calvin's insistence upon harder work for all his sons. Yet Rafe continued in his rakish ways. Two years later Ella bore a second child, which she said was his, and he did not deny it. This time, however, she did not "swear it," perhaps being mindful that Squire Winstead's sense of justice would not extend to salving her virtue twice.

Joe, the second son, was different from Rafe in his lack of

Uncle Calvin and His Five Sons

daring, or else he had a bit more discretion. He seemed to feel that his elder brother furnished enough of notoriety to his family. His comment was apt to be: "Jes' look at dat Rafe, ain't he a sight!" This cryptic remark would leave Joe's hearer uncertain whether it was made in general condemnation or admiring applause. Certainly he deferred to Rafe. This deference fell short in only one particular—he insisted upon his choice of the mules the family worked. His preference fixed upon the blazed-faced one—a rather rare mark in a mule. This animal had plenty of devil in his composition, but he and Joe formed an alliance that was workable and lasting.

Dave, the third son, was named at his birth by Cousin Delphia for the King of Israel. But unlike that spirited and self-made ruler, Dave proved to have no interesting qualities. He was dumb like the ox that trod out the grain. He required no muzzle but often a prod. While all Dave's brothers were full black like Uncle Calvin, he was copper-colored, like Aunt Harriet. But this was the sole characteristic of his mother's that he possessed. She was energetic and had a passion for neatness. Dave was sluggish in mind and body and always slovenly. He especially detested shoes and would never have worn any, winter or summer, had his mother not insisted when freezing weather came on. His feet seemed immune to cold and he regarded covering them a bother. Nor do I now believe he would have been the worse had he had his way—come sunshine, wet, or frost.

If Dave was one sort of trial to Aunt Harriet, Little Daniel was quite another. This boy was wiry and quick—quick in his movements and in all his decisions. He was combative in disposition and strongly inclined to resist correction. He "talked back" to his parents despite the threat of Uncle Calvin's switch which was sometimes well-laid-on at Aunt Harriet's insistence. She had set herself the task of making Little Daniel into a "good boy" after the quality of his Biblical namesake. But I am sure Little Daniel would have fought the lions rather than wait an attack. He was quick to fight with other young bucks, including his brothers. He kept the dull Dave in fear, and even Rafe and Joe walked warily when Little Daniel was "het up."

He had a competitive spirit as well as a combative one. He loved to wrestle in the country style. This sport involved a stand-up procedure, the wrestlers clasped breast to breast. The skill lay in the manipulation of legs and feet, with tricks of the body, to the end of hurling your opponent from you, prone on the sod. The rules and the jargon of the sport in the countryside were quite different from the wrestling art today.

Little Daniel loved to jump fences. I think he might have made a star track man. Our fences then were the "snake" variety, made of rails such as Lincoln was adept at splitting. These rails were laid up as high as you desired the fence to be. For horse and cow pastures the average was about five feet; for mules or fence-jumping cows greater heights were required. Little Daniel competed with the stock in the fence-jumping art. He evoked from his mother the sad prophecy that "dat limmer ain't gwine stay in no pastur!"

This prediction of Aunt Harriet soon came true. Little Daniel slipped the noose before he was twenty. He was lured by independent wages offered by a farmer who had seen him at the tobacco market. He landed some forty miles from home in another county and Aunt Harriet mourned him as a strayed colt—which he was. Yet the sequel was fortunate. After several years rumor came back that Little Daniel had married, had settled down, and was doing well. Still later, perhaps ten years, word came that the truant Little Daniel still had his wife, and now six children. And, most astounding of all, he had bought a small farm, for which he had well-nigh paid.

Edmund, the youngest son, like Little Daniel, had been born at our place in the double log cabin. He was not held to as consistent work as were his brothers. Perhaps I had something to do with the matter. Edmund was only three years older than I, and he made an excellent playmate. He hadn't much initiative and took most of his cues from me. Sometimes this led him into "situations," but none that was fatal. One, nearly so, was the result of an order to ride a scrub bull first—to gentle him for me. This led to a pitch that grounded Edmund twelve feet from the beast. Fortunately the toss was toward the fence. The boy made a run and a jump that Little Daniel would have praised as being "some jump."

In the summer season Edmund and I fished at the fishing "holes" on the South Hyco. He was often afraid we would meet Captain Robert Williams, who fished the same stream. Captain Robert had a rough humor with Negro boys when he had had a stout drink. Edmund held that the Captain would surely drown him some day in the deepest hole in the river. But this never happened and the edge of his fear gradually wore off.

In my memory is a particular summer day. My mother had given me reluctant permission to take Edmund and go fishing. With many an injunction and a small basket of lunch, we set off. Aunt Harriet had contributed several slices of bacon and the loan of her frying pan. At the stream Edmund peered up and down to assure himself the Captain wasn't near. Then we settled down to fish. Mud-cats were the best we had caught when our stomachs struck. Edmund kindled a fire while I cleaned our catch. I feared to trust him with that task, though he was fourteen and I was eleven.

The fish and bacon we fried together to shorten the time. We spread the food between us on paper. Then, feeling something lacking and remembering the custom at home, I ordered Edmund to "say grace." Edmund braced, closed his eyes, dropped his chin on his chest and uttered: "Amazing grace, how sweet the sound, that saved a wreck like me." I knew something was wrong about that grace! I half-suspected that "wreck" should be "wretch"; but I was so hungry from the smell of the fish I decided to let the version stand. Besides, Edmund had "blessed" in such solemn good faith!

Moreover, Edmund's rendering of "grace" snatched from a church hymnal, was not wholly out of abysmal ignorance. He was the one son Aunt Harriet still dragged with her to preaching at Hyco Zion, the nearest Negro church. She also took him with herself and Uncle Calvin to the Sergeants for a visit and dinner on every fourth Sunday. Before leaving for home in the late afternoon she would request Cousin Delphia for a

Bible reading. In summer this rite took place on the lawn under a shady tree; in winter in the kitchen, where Aunt Harriet had usually superseded the cook in the preparation of the Sergeants' Sunday dinner.

On one occasion in early June I begged permission of my mother to join the trio, and Aunt Harriet backed my plea. My mother and Cousin Delphia were great friends, having been girls together. Cousin Delphia was tall and stately and had beautiful brown eyes. Her hair was now quite white, but full and long. She had never married. She and her brother, Uncle John, long since a widower, were growing old together at the old home. My mother knew Cousin Delphia was fond of me and perhaps this was the main reason she gave me permission to go. Anyway I went, Edmund and I racing far ahead of Aunt Harriet and Uncle Calvin along the woods path. Somewhere, near midway, back in the woods, I could hear Aunt Harriet's voice, singing "Blessed be the tie that binds." When we arrived at the Sergeants, Cousin Delphia greeted us all and did not seem surprised to see me of the party.

The day went fine. I ate a tremendous dinner with Uncle John and Cousin Delphia—after a proper grace from Uncle John. I was quite sure Edmund was faring equally well with his parents in the kitchen. It was well past mid-afternoon when I laid myself open to a social misadventure. Uncle John and Cousin Delphia had had their naps. Uncle Calvin and Aunt Harriet walked about and sat under the trees, chatting with the cook. Here they had spent nearly the first half of their lives, and here their first three sons had been born. One intuitively knew that the friendship between them and the Sergeants was deep and sincere.

Edmund and I had played about quietly during the Sergeants' nap, warned by Aunt Harriet to make no noise. For the most part we played down at the barn, quite a distance from the house grove. We returned about the time the Sergeants came out on the lawn. Cousin Delphia now disclosed a special treat. She gave me a small pail and directed Edmund and me to fill it with strawberries from the garden. I had wondered about strawberries at dinner when dessert came on, knowing it was

Uncle Calvin and His Five Sons

strawberry time. But the rich egg custard Aunt Harriet had made had then knocked strawberries out of my mind.

Edmund and I returned in record time, the pail heaped up. I remember today Cousin Delphia's half-quizzical smile as she looked at my berry-stained face. Edmund, too, saw the look and immediately confounded me with his claim: "I never et a wun!" I was crestfallen and ashamed. Still I noticed my bowl was as full as any when Aunt Harriet and the cook returned with the berries from the kitchen, where they had been capped, sugared, and distributed in bowls, with cream poured over. Yet I had a guilty conscience even after the Bible chapter had been read and we had departed for home. I kept reflecting that Edmund was more virtuous than I—and doubtless he was.

As noted before, Aunt Harriet was neat and cleanly and struggled with her boys to make them so. Here she had indifferent success except with Rafe, who was something of a dandy. With Dave, she totally failed. But in her own room, and with Uncle Calvin, she achieved success. She was always scrubbing the floor, the mantel, or the hearthstones. Uncle Calvin complained that he would "ketch" cold from so much wet. Still she scrubbed. Uncle Calvin chewed tobacco, but was not allowed to spit in the fire.

Uncle Calvin and his sons liked ash-cake. This was a bread made by mixing corn meal with water and shaping it into a pone. The ashes were drawn aside, and it was laid on the hot stones and covered over with ashes to bake. The bread came out with a thick crust. Washed immediately it dried quickly from the inner heat. It was then an excellent and nourishing loaf. Eaten fresh with a cup of buttermilk it was a prince among breads. I shared in many a piece at Aunt Harriet's hands.

Out of this form of baking grew Aunt Harriet's rule against spitting in the fire. She forced Uncle Calvin to keep a sandbox when he chewed in the house, and to change the sand every so often. She had caught the idea of germs, an invisible pest then new to us all. "How you know dem jirms won't git in our bread" she would argue. "I 'spects dey gwine eat up dem boys in de yuther room anyhow!"

She had her way in her fight with germs, at least in her own room. Aunt Harriet, curious to note, was quite ahead of her time in her interest in germs. Quite some years later I thought of her when I heard a sermon by the last clerical head of a college which has since become a great university, noted for its interest in science. This ecclesiastic, who was later a bishop, denounced all innovations. "They now talk about germs," he proclaimed. "Germs! *I* eat 'em!"

Uncle Calvin farmed mainly tobacco on the land allotted to him and his "force." He had energy and courage to clear new land for his crop; a little each year. In fall and winter he and his sons would fell the trees and split up the timber for firewood and tobacco curing. Then they burned the brush, leaving the land clean of all save the larger stumps. In the early spring they coltered the land with a "bull-tongue" plow hitched to the two strong mules. This broke the soil and brought the roots to the surface, torn and broken. These would be grubbed out with mattocks and the soil turned again. When April came they made the rows; and early May saw the setting of the plants. This fresh soil, containing all the humus of long-decaying leaves, was just right for production of a good grade of tobacco. And it required very little commercial guano, an item which was quite expensive.

Uncle Calvin's tobacco was usually the best on the place. He cultivated it well. Besides, he produced some corn on the Hyco bottoms; and a few acres of wheat on "resting" tobacco land. "I aims to make my bread," he would say, and in this my father encouraged him. Some croppers would insist on planting only tobacco and depend upon this to pay for food the landlord furnished.

Marketing the tobacco in fall and winter was the climax of the tobacco year, though the process was a gradual one. In right condition the tobacco was packed in wagons of the schooner type and hauled long distances to auction markets. Each wagon carried a load of about a thousand pounds. This amount was held fair to a good team of horses or mules when one considered the rough and ungraded roads of the time.

In the last half of the decade of the eighties and the first year or two of the nineties, the vagaries of tobacco prices allowed the dawn of a little hope for tobacco areas. Landlords, tenants, sharecroppers, and wage hands all felt the stimulus.

It was in these years that I grew old enough to go to market with the wagons. Custom was for several wagons to journey together, neighbors joining to make up a group. Ours usually joined with wagons from the Sergeants and Uncle Ben Brookses. Will Brooks, my cousin, a half dozen years older than myself, was quite responsible and seemed always glad to have me along. One or the other of our fathers, usually mine, would travel in a buggy, behind a horse, and make the distance within the day. Will and I would come on more slowly with the wagons, each driven by a Negro man or a boy.

The distance to our chief market (at present a great tobacco town) was some thirty-five miles. This involved one camp on the road at night. This camp we would make preferably by a spring near the roadside or at the crossing of a stream. The tired stock would be watered, fed, and tethered to the tails of the wagons. One Negro would make a fire. Will and I would fry bacon and then scramble eggs in the hot bacon fat. I remember once breaking eggs in the sizzling fat as Will stirred with a long-handled spoon. In went a badly over-ripe egg before its condition was noted. Will's quick strokes buried the bad egg in with the good. I grunted and stopped; but Will "shushed" me and I broke in one more egg—our last. Only Uncle Calvin had seen as he tended the fire. His eyes twinkled, though he said nothing. And I noted he rejected eggs when they were tendered a little later. Perhaps he at last took seriously Aunt Harriet's education in germs. Will and I also refrained from eggs on that occasion, Will giving as our reason that there were only enough for the hungry drivers. Fourteens eggs had gone into the pan and they were all eaten by two men and a boy, with proportionate amounts of bacon and warmed-over bread.

Uncle Calvin cared little about going to market for the excitements of travel or a sight of the town. Rather I think he somewhat dreaded the break in his routine at home. Yet he liked to see his own tobacco sold. Nevertheless he often had occasion, when his piles of good tobacco had received their last bid, to remark to my father: "Marse Clem, hit didn't bring nigh enuf." But there was little he or Marse Clem could do about it. It was to accept the bid or re-load and haul the tobacco the long way home again.

After marketing tobacco Uncle Calvin never desired "settlement" for his share until he was again back home. If he needed a little money for immediate purposes he borrowed from my father. Rafe said this habit was due to fear of being robbed on the journey back, when he slept another night by the road. Rafe even told tales to support his point, tales that may, or may not, have been true. One was to the effect that Uncle Calvin slept with his head in a bucket on the journey back, this to prevent being clubbed. Another of these stories turned on the habit of market-bound haulers hailing market returners to learn "how tobacco was selling" (that is, at what average price). Rafe claimed that his father would reply that "tobaccy is selling so-so, but Marse Clem has got de money and gone on home." I never heard Uncle Calvin make this reply and never saw him sleep with his head in the horse-bucket. But I usually made the return trip with my father in the buggy. And I half believe that Rafe's stories were largely predicated upon rejections of his plea for money while in the town, money that Rafe would foolishly waste.

Uncle Calvin did have one peculiarity about money that my own observations verified and that caused my father a minor inconvenience. He would demand hard money in making "settlement." My father, to meet this whimsy, would procure silver money in a powder sack before leaving the town and thus be ready for settlement with him the day after he reached home. I have seen the old man receive as much as one hundred and sixty dollars from a sale—all in bright silver dollars. Later I saw him, after his noonday meal, sitting flat on Aunt Harriet's clean floor and stacking these dollars in ten-dollar piles. Rafe said he slept with the sack of money under his head, on the back side of the bed, Aunt Harriet in front. I did not believe this, either. He certainly cared for "Haret" and was always deferential toward her.

I never knew what arrangements Uncle Calvin had with his sons after they became of age. At twenty-one years they were legally independent and could have gone their own way—hired out for wages, or even become croppers, provided a landowner would trust their steadiness and industry. But Uncle Calvin's sons remained with him—all except Little Daniel. Joe hired out a year or two and then returned. Rafe, I think, liked the indulgence he had from his parents and disliked to subject himself to a new master. Also, I saw him with money now and then, after the debt for Ella's child had been paid off. Dave would naturally remain; and Edmund was young and always biddable—especially by Aunt Harriet.

After twenty-six years at our place Uncle Calvin and family moved back to the Sergeants. The surface reason was frivolous; the real reasons were understandable. The couple was getting old. Both were now quite grey. Their hearts had never been weaned away from the old attachments and they said "Miss Delphy" needed them—and this was doubtless true. Uncle John had been dead some years and his sister was now quite lonely.

But to make the change from our place called for an assignment of offence. This was found in an innovation brought in by my father. Custom had long been in our community to wind a horn to call the workers up in the morning and to call the noon hour when they were off in the fields. Now father brought home a large copper bell and mounted it on a twenty-foot post near the barn. It was rung by a rope that hung from an attached lever. Its notes could be heard for miles around.

Uncle Calvin did not like the bell. "I Gowd suh, I ain't no cow"; he proclaimed. His reference was to the custom of a belled cow to lead the cattle home. So he moved to the Sergeants, where they still wound a horn—though there he could still hear our bell both morn and noon.

We did not lose interest in the family after they moved and they still sometimes came to see us. The summer following the move in the fall we heard that Uncle Calvin was stricken with typhoid. My father went to see him and to consult with Cousin Delphia and Aunt Harriet. They provided a doctor, who came several times a week from the town. Aunt Harriet's care was unremitting.

He finally grew convalescent. The doctor enjoined that this was a critical period, and ordered a semi-starvation diet—a small bowl of soup with crumbs of bread mixed in. But Uncle Calvin's emaciated body cried out for food. Aunt Harriet was adamant for the doctor's orders. Uncle Calvin grew canny. He said he would rest better at night on a pallet on the floor. Aunt Harriet yielded to the seemingly innocent whim. Here he tossed restlessly about until his wife's tired body was dead asleep on her bed. Then he quietly crawled to the cupboard in the corner of the room. There he found an unbroken ash-cake and a pitcher of buttermilk. He ate the whole and crawled back to his place.

In the morning Aunt Harriet missed the food and was immediately aghast with suspicion and fear. She sharply questioned her mate and the answer she had was: "Ain't I done tole yo' all I needs is sumpin' to eat?" Aunt Harriet began to think on a suitable shroud, but Uncle Calvin's progress was continuous.

In the fall he was back at work with his "force" clearing new ground on the side of the road near Thaxton's Gate. He had begun this clearing the fall before. About three acres a year was his rate of progress against the long parallelogram of pines on the Sergeant side of the road. He still had Rafe, Dave, and Edmund, the latter now a full grown man. Rafe was nearing fifty years. He lived mostly with Ella and her still increasing family. Joe was working for wages at our farm. Edmund kept the garden and did the chores at Cousin Delphia's. Sometimes he worked in the fields with his father. The good news was just now arriving about the runaway Little Daniel.

Three years later, after Christmastime, I was returning to college for my last half-year, an experience I had had in some part due to Uncle Calvin and his family. By the road toward Thaxton's Gate I saw Uncle Calvin and his "force" over in the latest clearing, mauling up pines. I left the road and went over to greet them, to say good-bye. We chatted awhile. I spoke of great men. I had been studying history. I mentioned

Uncle Calvin and His Five Sons

Gladstone and Bismarck, both of whom had died the previous year. I told Uncle Calvin how Gladstone liked to fell trees and maul up the timber.

The old white-haired man leaned on his axe, listening attentively. He gazed up the length of the clearing and said "Dem was right peart men. But me, it tuk me five years to come fum right up yonder"!

At the end of winter I heard from home that Uncle Calvin had passed. They found him at the clearing, where he had gone ahead of his sons. I sent Aunt Harriet messages. When I returned in early summer I soon trod the old woods path to visit her. She was brave. In recounting the virtues of her departed mate she remembered her remaining blessings. "I still got Miss Delphy and most uv my boys," she said.

As I walked the shadowed woods path homeward even my young mind, with a college degree to lend a little courage, knew that an old century was now passing out.

Abimelech Matthew Jordan, Colporteur

The subject of this bit of reminiscence was a colporteur. His name was Abimelech Matthew Jordan. Lest the casual or indifferent reader be puzzled by a term that will pose the choice between ceasing to read, or resorting to a lexicon, it is well to explain at the start what a colporteur was. I use the past tense for the reason that this type of person, and his profession, has long since passed out—become obsolete, so to speak—at least in that part of the country where I was reared and where in my childhood I knew Abimelech Matthew Jordan.

The Southern Methodist Church up to the close of the past century had never found an effective way to ease the last years of its aged and outworn ministers. Practice was to keep them on long after their strength and powers had greatly declined and, when the very last dregs of service had been drained, to place them on the "superannuate list," with little or no provision made for their remaining years of life. Very few of the ministry had themselves possessed skill or opportunity to lay up a store of resource for this inevitable period—a period that comes to all men. And particularly did the Methodist ministry seem inhibited from concern about the future during the period of their strength. They had devoted themselves to a "high calling," many of them served heroically, all held the theory that the laborer was worthy of his hire, that the Lord and their congregations would provide. This was generally, though meagrely, true for the most as long as they could acceptably serve. But the time for the "superannuate relation" was a dread time when it came and often imposed the burden of their exhausted years upon their offspring in case any or all of these could insure protection. True, some of the territorial areas of the church known as "conferences," had got around before the end of the century to making meagre provision in the form of a dole from "Conference funds." Yet this was always uncertain, small, and quite inadequate to the needs of recipients.

Another device of the church that had arisen in an earlier period, and for long remained institutional, was to commission the superannuated minister to peddle bibles, approved religious tracts, collections of sermons, and song books used in church services. In this role he was called "conference colporteur." The theory was that he was still doing the work of the Lord. He had a wide field over which to roam, and his influence as shepherd of the sheep was still brought to bear.

At a much earlier day regular ministers still in the harness and serving a "circuit" of an over-burdening number of churches, also had often sold bibles, tracts, and hymnals to their flocks, and thus made out small and much needed additional income. In colonial New England, as is well known, the Puritan ministry also served as the dispensers of grog, gin, rum, and later whiskey, this on the theory that their moral influence would serve as an effective deterrent to abuse. Also there was the practical advantage that the profit accruing to the pocket of the clergy would relieve parishioners in proportionate degree from direct assessment for church support.

So frank and practical a relationship as the New England custom never became current in Southern Methodism. Even the sale of bibles, church literature, and hymnals by the "preacher" came to be thought unseemly before the end of the last century. A morning or evening sermon once a month at each of his churches seemed burden enough if the task was to be well done. And to this was to be added the "week of revival" at each church in the summertime. Also, perhaps the role of salesman, even of church literature, to a reluctant buying public was a handicap to the preacher who needed the favor of his flock in a steady relationship.

Hence, the rise of the colporteur, whose place and position in the scheme of things Methodist was compounded of several influences. It continued the distribution of church literature among a public which needs must be prompted in its consumption. It gave honorable employment to an outworn, and sometimes misfit, preacher who cared to assume this relation to the organization (conference). It was in keeping with the general idea of "itinerancy" fixed in Methodist polity.

Abimelech Matthew Jordan, the subject of this reminiscence, was a bit off type of the usual Methodist colporteur. He had not been retired from the high calling of the active ministry by virtue of age or physical decrepitude, but for other reasons unspecified. He had entered the ministry as a licensed preacher after long persistence at the door of the conference in urging the authenticity of his call by God to extend His kingdom. A puzzled bishop, perhaps a bit misguided by a still more puzzled presiding elder (a supervisor of a district composed of a large number of "stations" and "circuits"), had finally yielded to Jordan's importunity, and he had been licensed to preach. This was when he was about thirty-five years old. He had thereupon been assigned as preacher to a modest and backward circuit. But even there he proved to be sufficiently sub-standard to make the going hard, both for himself and his churches. God had called him but had not enlightened him effectively. Nor was his ambition to preach geared up to a will to learn. He had no aptitude for or interest in study. A slight acquaintance with the Holy Bible was the extent of his literary conquests. From this he had gathered a few aphorisms and quotations that he could use somewhat glibly. Besides this he had learned a good many names of Old Testament characters and a bit about the quality of some of these. Had he been a scholar he would probably have prospered best in the subject of genealogy.

After a four-year infliction of Abimelech upon the obscure circuit, information had gone up to the constituted authorities that he lacked the makings of a preacher, even for backward communities. What to do with him became the question. Revoking his license had awkward angles. It would be admission of careless judgment by the licensing authority. Precedent was also against revocation. Besides, Abimelech would be discouraged and blasted. Tact was needed to correct such an unusual situation.

But it had so occurred that the old colporteur of the district had just now died. Abimelech might be given this field for service to the church and thus none of the proprieties would be outraged. So Abimelech Matthew became colporteur at the early age of forty. He seemed to like the change and entered upon the new activity with a deal of interest. Already he possessed the first essential—a dilapidated horse and buggy used in his former circuit-riding. The kindly elder of the district assembled his first stock of spiritual literature and worked out for him a sales price-list. Then he took to the road as colporteur and for many years was a familiar figure in ours and adjoining conference areas of the country side.

No one would ever have acclaimed our colporteur as a business success. He was not fired with any particular zeal to push the business. But he liked the role, the passing lazily from one farm-house to another, the courteous reception because he was still a "reverend," the living on the country without charge because of this, and the constant change of scenes and contacts. He was conscientious in offering his wares for sale, but he was not an aggressive salesman. If no one bought he was not put out. If he effected a sale he was convinced the boundaries of the Kingdom had been slightly enlarged. He was always courteous in a simple way. He took himself just seriously enough to evoke a tolerant courtesy on the part of others. He expected and received the usual hospitality accorded preachers by the countryside. There was never any charge for his lodging and meals for either horse or man. Yet when forced by night or the exigencies of weather to lodge with a non-Methodist household, Abimelech generally offered payment in cash, not in spiritual literature. Particularly did he urge payment if he lodged with a Baptist. He said he did not wish to be beholden to Baptists. He seemed not to like this sect, having a dim conviction that their tenets were faulty.

Our country section was in the edge of this colporteur's area of travel. He did not reach it often. Probably once or twice a year he made his appearance at my boyhood home, generally in the summertime or early autumn. He was likely to arrive at the time of our week of revival, staged in the middle of the summer, when the crops had been well worked up and the harvest period had not yet begun.

Abimelech Matthew Jordan enjoyed the atmosphere of the revival and was quite at home in it. He liked both the spiritual tensions and the physical relaxation, apparently finding them in no way at clash, but rather complementary one to another. He ate gargantuan dinners, often passing from one table to another to sample their food, and finding a welcome at each. Then with the first peal of church music, signalling the opening of the afternoon service, he would pass into church. There he would take his place in the "Amen Corner" and be ready to punctuate with hearty amens the opening prayer. When "mourners" were called for at the end of the sermon, Abimelech took his place behind the altar and in husky and emotional undertones pointed the way to sinners through the mystic process of conversion. He would lead in simple but somewhat perfervid and lurid prayer when called on by the preacher in charge.

After services Abimelech would expect and receive an invitation for the night from some head of a family, over against a return next day. Though he had his colporteur's stock of spiritual literature along, both at church and in the houses he visited during the revival week, he pushed the commercial end not at all. He seemed to sense that money transactions, even in sacred literature, would place him in the seat of a money changer at the door of the Temple, and so deprive him of the dignity of a worker in souls.

Once my father, prompted by my mother as a matter of duty, invited Abimelech to spend the night with us. Then a ten-year-old boy, I rode with him in his colporteur's rig, behind his raw-boned bay horse, from the church to my father's home. At the beginning of the ride I was in a chilly sweat. I feared he would talk to me about Hell, the kind of Hell I had heard him picture in his prayers at church—a kind of place greatly to be avoided. But much to my relief, when out on the road, he seemed to revert to the familiar world I knew. He spoke about birds and their songs and said he liked to see and hear them. He asked how many kinds of birds I knew and whether I knew them by sight or song. It gave me confidence that I knew more of our feathered friends than did he. When we crossed the bridge over the small river near my home he asked about the fish in the stream, what kinds they were, whether I was allowed to go fishing by myself, and whether I could swim. All this was such sure and familiar ground to me that I forgot about Hell and was quite at ease with him by the time we arrived. I assisted him in unhitching his horse and led it to water at the well. There the horse drank so thirstily that I dared preach the colporteur a little sermon of my own. It was hesitant but heartfelt. It suggested sin, the sin of people at church who sometimes kept their horses tied to a tree all day without either food or water. The colporteur agreed with my general position, but pointed out that there might be more important things to attend to at church, things of the spirit for instance. I took alarm at this point and led the horse off to the stables and food.

I had a keen curiosity to observe and measure my father's reactions to Abimelech Matthew Jordan, and so hung about as they sat in chairs drawn out on the lawn after supper. My father was not a religious zealot in any sense. This I had already noted in the heat of revivals at church. He kept his feet on the ground, and his measurement of people and things were, to me, something like final judgments. Hence in this role of host to the colporteur I did not expect him to talk religion. Yet there had to be talk to make the situation easy.

First, I noted my father called him "Jordan," while I had been puzzled about my form of address. I had alternated between "Mr. Jordan," and "Mr. Ab," having heard some people call him the latter at church. My father called him "Jordan" in an entirely natural way and asked him about his Christian names. The colporteur repeated them in full— "Abimelech Matthew."

"You see my mother named me that-a-way. She was a Christian woman and wanted me to have one foot in each Testament. Abimelech," he went on, apparently relishing the subject of names, "was a king. I have looked him up. He was good to Isaac, Abraham's son, when Isaac and his wife were on a trip through the country where this king lived. Some folks, when they hear me called 'Ab,' think I was named after 'Abner,' which I wasn't. Abner was not a king. He was the servant of a king, a sort of first servant, who had charge of the army. He was a man of blood. He was in David's time. But he weren't at first on David's side. Abner held to Saul's son when Saul died. That son was named Ishbaal. Most folks wanted David to be the king. After awhile Abner went over to David's side. But Joab, David's man of war, was jealous and killed him. Maybe it served him right. I don't believe in being first on one side and then on another.

"Matthew," continued the colporteur, "you know about. I regard him as the best of the apostles, though Peter was more outspoken. Peter was weak in the knees when he got in a pinch. But I guess his heart was always in the right place. My mother liked Matthew best. He wrote one of the Gospels. She uster read from that more than any other when she read in the New Testament; though she read in the Old Testament most. My father didn't like for her to read the Bible at all."

"Why not?" my father asked rather idly, as if to make conversation and to keep Abimelech going. I soon sensed that he regretted the diversion in this direction. Not so with Abimelech. He took up the thread with no embarrassment. "My father," he said, "was not a Bible man. In fact he was wicked, and saw no sense in religion. He would rather get drunk, when he could find the money. He was a cropper over in Caswell County. He always came home drunk when he sold his tobacco. He said it was the only pleasure he had. He could not read, not even the Holy Word. My mother tried sometimes to read to him, but he would not listen. She taught me to read and I have always been glad. There is a power of comfort in having some learnin'. My father died first and I looked after my mother as best I could till she was gone too. She always wanted me to preach. She said the Lord would show a way. I tried hard and finally got licensed, long after my mother was dead. But I guess I wasn't a very good preacher, though the people were good to me on the one circuit I had. Then I was made colporteur, and I guess that is one sort of preaching."

My father conceded it was, and suggested that perhaps it was time to go to bed. Abimelech agreed and I was relieved to note no suggestion was made as to a "word of prayer." Even so I had a bad night—an unusual thing for me. I dreamed fitful and lurid dreams, mostly about drunks on the way from market and journeying toward a place called Hell. Looking back I am uncertain of the cause—whether a little toe-hold on the preaching I had heard at the revival, or a big stomach-hold on the ham and cake I had garnered there.

My next contact with Abimelech, the colporteur, lingers in my memory in even sharper outline than does my picture of him at revivals and of his first visit at my home. This contact led to a second visit and spending the night, though this time without formal invitation except by me.

I was travelling barefoot along a hot and dusty road toward my home, about two miles distant. This road, like all roads of the period in our countryside, was a friendly and intimate road. It wandered along without reference to the laws of a surveyor's transit. It sought the easiest gradients along the course of a brook, or a larger stream. It dallied along through the shade of timbered stretches. It almost seemed to pause as it passed near a copious spring. Here it seemed to invite the passerby to rest and refresh himself and beasts. Later it must needs climb up over a great high hill and wind down on the other side; and so on to its goal. This afternoon, in the heat of summer, and despite the rumblings of heavy thunder from a great black cloud spreading up from the west, I turned aside along a foot path to a cool spring I knew, some fifty yards from the road. This spring was an ever-flowing one, even in drought-time. It was in the midst of a grove of great trees—oak and hickory and sycamore giants. Underbrush was absent and green grass had found a chance to grow.

Approaching this spring I saw an old and dispirited mule tied by his halter to a hitching staple in one of the trees. This mule was unfamiliar, but soon I saw near by the colporteur's rig, which I recognized. Looking further I saw Abimelech

Matthew Jordan, dead asleep on a well-shaded plot of grass just above the bubbling spring. I slaked my thirst from a gourd that lay on a stone by the spring and puddled my feet for a moment in the cool water below. Then I was warned anew by the dark shadow of the cloud, the heavy thunder, and the great streaks of lightning blasting the clouds. Should I wake the sleeper and share in the drenching that was now assured, or should I make a hot run for it to a house at the top of a great steep hill about half a mile further along? I decided to wake the colporteur, though I was half afraid he was dead, since he could not hear such thunder.

When awake he greeted me as friend. Then he observed the cloud and said we had probably better get away from there, since lightning sometimes struck large trees. We put the mule to the rig. This animal showed no perturbation at all. He seemed to suggest that it was all in a day's experience. We mounted to the seat and Abimelech, with voice and light touches of the whip, urged the mule along toward the great high hill. This we reached, in tedious time, so indifferent was the pace of the mule. And here the storm broke in all its fury when we were about half-way up the heavy grade. The water came down in torrents; the lightning cracked in continuous succession. It was the lightning I feared. I think it reminded me of things I had heard in revivals.

In the midst of all the mule decided to go on strike. He was a "cold-shouldered" mule, with a fixed aversion to pulling to the top of a hill. For a time the colporteur urged and persuaded from his seat and applied his whip with increasing vigor— though he was a merciful man. I was already on the ground, trying to push from behind. I felt that this might give the mule a bit of encouragement. But it was to no avail. He would not move. He seemed to take it strange that he was expected to. The colporteur then tried leading him up the hill while I applied the whip. It would not work. The mule was determined not to go in that direction. Abimelech's tones grew increasingly acid. He began to address the beast in terms of abuse, while all the time the water poured as if from buckets. I could scarcely hear, though I caught the gist of Abimelech's speech out of strained curiosity. I was anxious to know if Abimelech would swear. He did not, or else I failed to hear in the storm's uproar. But he called the balky mule the great-grandson of Balaam's ass, the wicked offspring of an unholy cross. "Blasted brute," he cried, "do you think to make a Baptist of me by keeping me here in all this flood?" The mule seemed impervious to the threat of sectarian humiliation for his master. He eyed the rest of the hill with sour disfavor, as if he would turn all things Baptist rather than pull.

Abimelech then had a thought. He slogged to the back of the rig and pulled out some bundles of tracts. He found some partially dry as yet, having been covered over with a tarpaulin. He produced some matches from a tin box he carried, though he was not a smoker. "Now," I thought, "Mister Jordan is going to give him Hell!" But Mister Jordan was, in soul, a humane man. In the very first lull in wind and rain he lit the papers into a hearty flame. I expected to see him apply the torch under the mule's belly, where the skin was tender. Instead he raised the tail and stuck it under. The mule was puzzled, but not for long. He showed real animation as he whirled in his tracks and overturned the rig. He started down the hill instead of up, bumping the vehicle along at every awkward jump. At the bottom of the hill the shafts broke off, the torch had been lost, or drenched out in the renewing rain. The mule had resumed his calm and had begun to crop wet grass by the roadside.

The worst was over now. Soon the sun came out and shone through the brilliant-hued edges of the after-clouds. I began to enjoy the scene. Wet to the very bones, we were not cold. In about half an hour the colporteur and I had picked up a bushel of tracts and sermons scattered down the hill from the point where he had lighted the blaze. Mercifully the bibles had escaped the wreck, being packed in a lidded box covered over in oil-cloth. Abimelech said the Lord looked after His own, and wondered who looked after mules.

I asked him where his horse was, why he was driving a mule. He said he met Bob Perkins the day before and Bob had bantered him for a trade. I knew Perkins as one of the shrewdest of the shrewd. He was the local trader in broken-down stock. He had human "psychology," my father said, and though the word was too big for me I knew its meaning. Perhaps Ed Perkins, Bob's son about my age, had given me my interpretation. Ed always boasted that "my Pap can trade off a sorry horse and git a good horse and money to boot! I b'leve he could trade off a dead horse and git a live horse and money to boot! I speck he could trade the eye-teeth out of the Philadelphy lawyer!" And truly I myself believed that Perkins could do all those things. My father's word "psychology" became linked in my mind with this trader and remained so many a year. Curiously, when I came to college as a young man, I there found that the lone professor of psychology was a sometime dealer in horse-flesh. More curious still, I had a disastrous transaction with him in which, for breeding purposes, he sold me a female jackass at a double price!

Next morning, when the colporteur had led his mule off to retrieve the wreckage of his rig, I told my father about the trade with Perkins. He chuckled and remarked: "Once a Greek met a blind barbarian." I have never seen or heard this quotation since. I think it was original with my father. And certainly I caught the meaning, without effort or strain.

After the incident of the mule and the storm I saw no more of the colporteur for three or four years. Then he re-emerged upon our stage in an interesting role. He became a lover and, in quick succession, a married man.

In our neighborhood, in fact upon my uncle's farm not far from ours, there lived a strange old woman named Betsy Boyd. She had appeared out of nowhere some half a dozen years before with a daughter named Jenny. The mother was strange in appearance and strange in her silence. The latter quality she had impressed upon her daughter. The mother was probably about sixty years old, with a stoop to her shoulders. With a long hooked nose and piercing black eyes set in her wrinkled face, she was the veritable embodiment of the witch we saw riding the broom in our fairy-tale books. The daughter was about thirty-five. She was tall and angular, possessing a good forehead but a very weak chin.

My uncle, on the understanding that Miss Jenny was a good

sewing woman, gave them a cabin near a spring in a grove of trees. His provident wife, Aunt Anne, would make good use of Miss Jenny in seasonal sewing for her family. Besides, she could go out to sew for other families in the neighborhood who had large flocks of children. "Miss Betsy" was given a small plot of land near the cabin where she could tend a garden for vegetables.

I came to know Miss Betsy, usually observing her at a distance, as I roamed over my uncle's place. She never went anywhere, had no contacts whatever, and seemed to care for none. I think I never heard her voice at all. But this may have explanation in the fact that I gave her wide berth when I had occasion to pass her cabin and spring.

Miss Jenny I knew in my mother's home where she early came to sew on clothes for our family. She would eat dinner with the family and return home at night. She was never talkative. My mother and sisters were too tactful to probe her, respecting her reserve. So we never came to know her background or whence she came. She was a good sewing woman and planned and made my eldest sister's wedding dress. I heard my sister say that Miss Jenny took a "pathetic" interest in this dress. But this may have been the concept of my sister's young and romantic mind.

Abimelech Matthew Jordan, the colporteur, stopped at Miss Betsy's spring upon a day when Miss Jenny was not out at sewing. He walked to the cabin to ask for the privilege of eating his lunch and feeding his horse by the spring. (He now had a horse in place of the balky mule.) Miss Jenny granted this privilege. Soon she walked down to the spring for a bucket of water. Incidentally she bore a goodly portion of nice fried chicken to add to the wayfarer's lunch. Abimelech detained her in conversation. He liked to talk. She liked to listen. Many things might have been his topic. He could have told her Bible stories. Perhaps he told her of Ruth and her gleaning in Boaz's field. Or, perhaps, he made a more immediate application of the story of Rebecca at the well. Certainly he was familiar with Rebecca's story, for it was the fortunate Isaac who made a covenant with King Abimelech of Gerar.

Whatever the alchemy that served as precipitant, the romance opened suddenly, like the night-blooming Cereus. Miss Jenny sewed at our home the next few days. She told my sisters she was "engaged," was to be married on a Sunday ten days hence. They were aghast but overjoyed, and asked wherefores. Miss Jenny contributed to their curiosity but meagrely. She showed them a neat new Bible, the fly-leaf inscribed in a sprawling hand: "To Jenny from Abimelech Matthew— August 26, 1894,—Near Concord Church." She had a new light in her usually tired eyes.

My sisters offered assistance in preparation. She said there would not be much need. She would go to church in the colporteur's rig, taking Miss Betsy along with them. They would be married at the end of the service.

This came about in the manner planned, Miss Betsy making a curious spectacle to the eyes of the young. She wore her slatted poke-bonnet, a dark calico dress with many a rumpled fold, and carried her hobble-stick I had always seen her with when not working with a hoe in her garden. She stolidly kept her seat in the back of the church when the bride and groom went forward at the end of the sermon. When the magic words had been said, and the preacher's voice had died, the groom himself uttered a loud and solemn "Amen!"

Several weeks later the trio went away to the western edge of Caswell County, where Abimelech had been born, and where he now rented a small place with intent to farm. It was supposed by us that Miss Jenny would continue her sewing.

These short annals of Abimelech Matthew Jordan, colporteur, end all my direct knowledge of the man and his life. Yet my interest once again was awakened by a startling aftermath. It was thirty years later that I met a man from the area to which Abimelech, his bride, and his mother-in-law had retired. I asked of them, curious to know the end of the tale. He told me all were long since dead, but that Abimelech and his wife had left a son, Jonathan David, who was killed in the Battle of the Argonne, 1918; that this son had been cited, posthumously, for exceptional bravery; that the Distinguished Service Cross had been awarded—with no one found to receive it.

The Quick-Witted Young Man

To plane off somewhat the sharp edges of the present I was just now thinking of my father and the period in which he grew to manhood. This was just before the Civil War.

That period now seems a long way back, and is. Yet through his eyes I got many a glimpse of a way of life soon, too, like ours, to be cast into the crucible of change.

My father had humor, but of its peculiar kind. He was never a punster or jokesmith. I never heard from his lips a pale and piddling joke, picked up second-hand, or from the thousandth repetition. His humor was serious humor. It emerged from his store of experience, from his observation of life and people. Sometimes, not often, he could laugh at himself. He told stories to his children but sparingly. Always they had a point. If they had humor it appeared incidental. For the point of his tale was a lesson about character, or action—not designed to evoke merriment, though it ofttimes did.

We, his children, knew his stories were always authentic, always illustrated some facet of life as he had known it, either in peace or war, and the humor was well cloaked over with matter for instruction. Such, for instance, was his story which, had he been impelled to name it, he would probably have called "The Haughty Young Woman," or "Pride Goeth Before a Fall." His children, girls and boys both, hearing him relate it only once, agreed to call it "The Quick-Witted Young Man." This seemed to us more suited, but probably because our sense of humor was distorted.

The tale came out one Saturday night, incident to my protest against riding a mule to Sunday School and church at fifteen years of age. Pride was the theme, and when my father began, I did not expect a story that would meet my point. And it hardly did, though in the end it slurred it over.

"When I was a boy," he began, "nearly everybody around here rode to church on horseback."

"Yes," I interrupted, "*horseback*, not *muleback!*"

"But Mike will get you there, and it is more how you do *after* you get there than *how* you get there!"

He continued: "I remember a young woman of this neighborhood when I was young, about your age myself. She rode horseback every Sunday to church, a nice, lively horse. She was pretty and spirited and had a good opinion of herself, rightly. But she was a bit hoity-toity and was choosy about which of the young men waited on her."

I already knew the meaning of the accustomed phrase: "waited on." In our community use, it had several connotations, depending upon the context. Here it meant an attentive young man coming forward when a young lady rider had drawn rein, offering one hand for her foot, the other for her hand, and so lighting her to the ground. Meanwhile the lady's disengaged hand rested with interested pressure upon the young gallant's shoulder.

"In this case," continued my father, "there was a young man, not popular with the young ladies, and particularly with this young lady. Yet he was eager to wait on her.

"One Sunday morning when the people were arriving, and many were already there, the young fellow placed himself in a favorable position near the spot where the young woman usually stopped her horse. She rode up, expecting some of her favorites to be near. They were; but the unpopular young man was nearest. She saw the situation, and, to avoid his services, she leaped from the side-saddle unassisted. In her haste the hem of her riding skirt caught on the pommel of the saddle. This stripped all her clothes up far too high.

"Undaunted by the emergency the unpopular young man did not hesitate. He clapped his hat over the broadest axis of exposure and cried out loudly: 'More hats here, young gentlemen! more hats! *More* hats, *please!*' "

Here my father stopped, at the belated headshaking of my

mother. But I, not liking to leave the young woman suspended while the additional hats arrived, requested to know what happened next.

"A more practical young man released the skirt and so righted the situation. But the young woman was less haughty thereafter. She seemed to settle down, treated everyone with due consideration. By-and-by she came to play the church organ, both for Sunday School and church. Later she married a widower from the Oak Grove neighborhood and raised his first wife's children and several of her own."

Wiley Buck

Wiley Buck had another name. On the south side of the river, where he came in season for occasional employment, he was "Major." His surname, if surname he had, was Winstead, acquired from the owner of his mother before the Civil War. But he was never called by this name, never claimed it, and nowhere was it found in any record of church, school, voter's register, or taxpayer's list. He was outside the orbit of these functioning activities, and they took no account of him. Only once did his entity appear in an official record—a court proceeding about a year before his gruesome end.

At the inception of this long-drawn-out and quite bewildering experience with the law, he stood before the bar charged with grave crime, a crime for which, if convicted, the penalty was death by hanging from the neck on Gallows Hill near the county seat. Asked his name on this occasion, he gave it as Wiley Buck. I believe he took a certain and definite pride in that name and in the way it had been acquired. His mother had called him Wiley at birth sometime just before the Civil War, but "Buck" had come to him in another way. Born on the south side of the river, he had shifted to the north side in early manhood. Here he found a situation more congenial. The population on this side was sparse and generally shiftless—both white and black. It was not particularly lawless, but tended to be shy and self-conscious on the rare occasions of his contact with the main current of the county's life.

The river itself, the Hycotee, was not a large or important stream. Nor was the Dan, into which it flowed. But when the Dan had reached the Roanoke their combined waters made up a broad, muddy, and somewhat sluggish flood before they entered Albemarle Sound which cut through the Carolina coastal plain from east to west. The Hycotee was in no way distinguished except that it divided the "north" from the "south" side in Wiley Buck's world, and once, with the Dan, divided the Carolina Tuscaroras from the Catawbas. There were no bridges or ferries on thirty-mile stretches of its course. This was because of rough and broken country on the north side and because few roads then existed there; while on the south side, where planter life had flourished in the middle of the century, the roads ran east and west with the river.

Wiley, a primitive by inheritance and nature, had early taken up residence on the north side in a log cabin not far from the river. This he had found unoccupied and situated quite away from immediate neighbors. It had been built and owned by a restless and drifting white who had long since left his holding to revert to the county in lieu of taxes. Here Wiley crept in and established himself. He felt no need of neighbors, seeming to prefer isolation from members of either race. His herd instinct found its limit in the ownership of dogs, for which he had a great and abiding love. Homeless dogs, crippled, sick, or mangy, big or little dogs, dogs so mixed that none could guess their ancestry—all found an instinctive friend in Wiley. He nursed them to lean and hungry health again and hunted them over the hills for rabbits by day and along the river bottoms by night for coons and possums. His hunting was always on the north side. He never allowed his dogs to cross the river, though many of them were garnered there. He sensed the hostility of the farmers to a foraging pack of hungry pillagers, and gave heed to their attitude.

Even so, game on his side of the river was the more plentiful and was on the increase. Unknown to Wiley, deer in small numbers were pushing back up the valleys of the Roanoke and the Dan from the swamp lands nearer the coasts. They moved up the Hycotee, along the north side of the river, where the country had reverted to bush and "second growth" pines, and where men were scarcer.

It was incident to this return of the deer that Wiley became "Wiley Buck." Wiley had never owned a gun at any time and never acquired one. He depended upon strategy and the manipulation of his pack. The day he became "Wiley Buck" he was out along the stream and the hillsides that crowded the narrow valley. His object was a rabbit drive for his hungry dogs. The mongrel group of some twenty dogs, out of Wiley's sight, raised something near the river that fled away through a draw in the hills and led them away out of hearing. Wiley was puzzled. He knew it wasn't a rabbit. A rabbit was a "short-ranger" and ran in an irregular circle from its starting point. Moreover, for rabbit Wiley had taught his pack to spread out. Now his pack had gone off in full cry bunched together. It could not be a big dog-coon; coons travelled by night and took to water when crowded. There they made a gallant fight. Wiley over the years had lost several of his dogs through water-fights with a tough old coon. This was one subject he would talk about on the rare occasions he ever encouraged me to join him at his fishing places along the river.

Coons ruled out, Wiley's conclusions was that a fox had led his pack away. And the fox was a form of unprofitable hunting for him, as proved in the past. He had never taken one. He trudged up the ridge expecting to meet the discouraged dogs straggling back. Instead, at the crest, he heard a far-distant baying that seemed stationary. "Treed," thought Wiley, and he made through the pines toward the increasing clamor. Arrived, he beheld a new sight to his eyes. A large buck deer stood at bay surrounded by the yapping pack. The animal's hind leg was freshly broken above the hock, an accident doubtless from an unlucky landing as he bounded through the jagged down timber. He still showed plenty of fight with his eight-point antlers. But Wiley was not to be denied. Here was the embodiment of a dream come true. His method of attack was forthright and primitive. Encouraging his dogs to close in, Wiley himself, from behind the nearest bush, leaped in and seized the buck by the antlers close in to the head. He held on and twisted. The dogs swarmed over the struggling pair. The deer's neck snapped under his inspired wrenches, and the victory was his.

Trudging over the hills toward his distant cabin, the prize

on his back, the slavering dogs at his heels, Wiley stopped to rest, and perhaps for a bit of quiet display, at a Negro cabin on his route. Here the awe-struck occupants stood around in honest amazement at the trophy and the hunter's prowess. Here he was christened "Wiley Buck."

No invitations were issued to a venison feast. Only Wiley Buck and his dogs shared in their common kill. And the front of the head, antlers proudly pointing, was nailed over the cabin door on the outside. There for months it competed in smell with the rotting skin on the roof. Both advertised the might of Wiley Buck to distant neighbors who made a journey to see whether rumor was true. So, the name "Wiley Buck" became permanent.

Still Wiley Buck's menage needed a bit more than the fruits of the chase, even though for once his larder had contained a hefty buck. Not clothes for either cover or warmth drove him across the river to the farms for an occasional few days' labor. His clothes requirements were easily satisfied with a cast-off pair of overalls, a tattered shirt, a mouldering hat or cap. Replacements could be had as had the originals: by exchange of a possum or a string of fish at one of the farms, when he crossed the river.

It was additional food that brought Wiley Buck across to our side. He made preparation in advance by inducing a sixteen-year-old Negro boy named Ed to stay at his cabin and keep his dogs together. His gift to Ed for this service was a pressed plug of tobacco and a bit of bacon on his return. At the farms he made his stay as brief as possible, rarely as much as a week, either winter or summer. The wages he required were not set in terms of money; a bag of corn meal, a half side of bacon, a jug of sorghum—or varying portions of these— were what he labored for. And it is probable that his dogs received more of his earnings than the laborer himself.

My father's farm was nearest where Wiley Buck usually poled his raft across the river. Here he would first apply for labor. If there was need for his unskilled services he was set to work—in summer hoeing tobacco or corn, in the autumn pulling fodder or gathering the corn. He nearly always appeared in late autumn or early winter at hog-killing time. He had a canny judgment as to when this event would take place, perhaps guided by a succession of heavy frosts. He was the first in the pen to grapple and throw a surprised and squealing porker. He was good at the scraping as the slaughtered hogs were drawn from the hot-water vat where their hair had been loosened. The night after hog-killing he always returned home well laden with a liver, a haslet (lungs), and maybe a whole hog's head in exchange for his labor.

It was in these labor expeditions of Wiley Buck that I came to know him, perhaps better than any other person except the boy Ed. His primitive look, his primitive manner of life, his ownership of a whole flock of dogs and—above all—the story of his exploit in killing the pioneer buck, fascinated my young mind. He talked little to either whites or blacks; but I hung about him at his work and persisted in questioning him to satisfy my curiosity. My imagination was fired and the north side of the river almost became repopulated with roving Catawbas.

Wiley Buck was very black, but not the shiny black of the average black Negro. Harking back to my memory picture of him I would describe his color as ash-black. His brow was heavy and his chin was square and firm. His eyes were pig-like and were blood-shot in the corners. His teeth stood rather far apart and were strong and white. His gums were bluish. His lips were thin, but his broad flat nose conformed to the African type. Not especially strongly built, Wiley Buck nevertheless gave the impression of reserved strength. About fifty years old when I first knew him, he had retained all the superstitions our part of the Negro world had inherited or produced. The unknown kept him in partial terror, and even the known was filled with the portents of danger. He was particularly antipathetic to crawling and creeping things. "Ah laks things dat move a little above de groun, not too high, not too low," he used to say to me. Frogs, snakes, lizards, scorpions, sand-skeeters, certain kinds of worms, and numerous kinds of flying bugs and beetles set his nerves on edge and produced reactions of avoidance. Bats were especially anathema. I have seen them drive him from his fishing as they flitted over the water toward the close of the day. All these things were either dangerous or unlucky, mostly dangerous.

I remember he had come for wheat-threshing late in a hot June. The wheat stood in tall stacks in an open field. The "thrasher" and crew were ready for action. My father ordered Wiley Buck (he was "Major" to us) up a fence rail to the top of the first stack. There he was to throw off the bundles of wheat to the "table" of the thresher, whence it was fed into the whirling machinery. Operations had scarcely begun when Major let out a weird scream, leaped the twelve or fifteen feet to the ground below, and made off yelling across the field. He tore at his ragged britches as he ran. Watchers thought he had gone suddenly daft. I alone guessed the truth: a harmless lizard had run up his britches' leg, and the contact had completely unnerved him. Finally he stumbled and fell and the lizard escaped through one of the many breaks in his clothes. But Major refused to remount that stack, or any other. He was put to raking straw and soon calmed down, and he came out of that experience the gainer—if you discount shocked nerves. My father gave him a pair of still serviceable trousers to replace what had passed for his britches, now beyond holding together again.

Wiley Buck got his name "Major," used on our side of the river, from the whimsey of a young man of our neighborhood named Johnny Williams. Young Williams had observed that all the Confederate "Captains" were in the rural areas around about and all the "Colonels" were in the county town. For example, Johnny's father was a demoralized ex-slaveowner known as "Captain" Bob Williams. And there was Captain Robert Sergeant, and Captain Tom Stephens, and several others by "courtesy" or military service. In the town were Colonel Rube Featherstone, Colonel Charles Winstead, Colonel John Cunningham, and perhaps a few others I do not recall. Young Williams held that the countryside should also have a ranking title. Thus he christened Wiley the "Major" long before I knew him, and this name was as permanent on our side of the river as Wiley Buck became on the other.

Major was in no sense social-minded. He seemed inhibited in making contacts with his own race. Whether this was due to an inferiority complex on his part, or was begotten of his own race's evident aversion to him, I never reasoned out—then, or since. But the estrangement was quite apparent, even to my immature observation. It showed in numerous small ways and on both sides. If put to work with other Negroes he worked apart, if conditions allowed. When mealtime came and the "hands" gathered at the farmer's kitchen, Major would ask for his share on a separate dish and retire apart to eat alone. Some of the Negroes spoke of him as "dat wild nigger," and showed dislike in petty ways. But these signs of dislike were not flaunted in Major's face in open fashion. I think they had a little fear, not proceeding from any quarrelsomeness, on Major's part, but rather from his silence; nor did his heavy brow and square-cut chin invite an open taunt.

Distrustful and silent, and generally self-repressed, Major nevertheless "fell into a pit" on our side of the river. It was the one instance in which he yielded to a normal impulse to bridge the gap between himself and others. It was by the world-old human route of temptation by an Eve.

The matter developed on a neighboring farm to ours, that of Captain Bob Williams. The Captain's acres, like the Captain himself, were greatly run down. He had no skill in management and less ambition to acquire the needed virtue. His "hands" were sharecroppers of the most thriftless and disreputable sort. The riffraff usually resorted to his place. Major had come over the river and, finding no labor at our place, had gone to the next nearest, that of Captain Bob. Here he had been taken for a few days' work at woodcutting. Here the stout black cook named Ellen was already possessed of several children whose fatherhood was known only to herself and God, or mayhap only to God. This cook, for the two days Major was there, piled his dish unusually high with black-eyed peas and hog jowl, a food of which Major was inordinately fond. Major accepted this gesture as a certain sign. It may have meant sympathy for one who walked alone; it could have meant one of several things. But to Major it was the call of primitive to primitive. The first night he had passed shivering in the scant hay in the barn; the second he knocked on the cook's door in the corner of the yard. There he found Ellen by a toasty fire with "'company"—two other Negroes of the place, one married, one not. Ellen's children were asleep in the loft.

Major "sat the company out." They later testified in open court that he became aggressive toward the hostess before they left. She later swore that Major made advances, that she slapped his face, that he still pushed his suit. Certainly as a climax she ran into the yard and squalled. Young Johnny was away, but Captain Bob rushed out of the "big house" with a rusty musket in hand. He heard the cook's tale, which was none too explicit, and ordered Major off the place at the point of an unloaded gun.

By testimony of the boy Ed, not rendered in court, Major reached his cabin before midnight. If so he must have covered the five miles distance in rapid time, with a river thrown in. The culminating incident at the Williams place was half past ten.

But this rapid withdrawal on the night of the incident was not material. What was material was that eight days later, the night before Thanksgiving, the cook's house was burned to the ground between three and four o'clock, Ellen and her children barely escaping with their lives.

The married visitor of the previous incident now came forward to report that he had been hunting a stray cow when dark overtook him, near the river; that he had seen Major land from his raft and slip through the pines towards the Williams place. The second visitor swore that, aroused from sleep by the clamor over the fire, he rushed toward the blaze, that on his way he saw by the glow a man dart into the pines from behind the barn. This man he swore he recognized as Major.

The loop was now practically about Major's neck. The crime was arson, if crime was committed. The penalty was hanging if the crime was proven. Captain Bob believed his Negroes' stories. Ellen took no side. She may have recalled she was notably careless with fire. Major was arrested and given a preliminary hearing. Knowing nothing of the device called an "alibi," and as little of the calendar a week old, he merely maintained he had not crossed the river since the night of his retreat before Captain Bob's gun. The prosecution's charge that Major was guilty seemed plausible to the committing magistrate, Squire John Banks Bradsher, Captain Bob's brother-in-law. Major, therefore, was remanded to jail to await trial for his life at April term of court.

Never before had the prisoner been to the county town. There he resided behind bars for the next six months. The jailer said his chief concern seemed to be about some dogs and the whereabouts of a boy named Ed. But Ed likewise had never traveled as far as the town, some seventeen miles from where he lived. And Major, having no friends, had no emissaries to send to Ed about his dogs. The dogs proved too much responsibility for the boy. They soon broke up and scattered to take their individual chances for food.

My father slowly formed the opinion that Major was innocent. I swore that he was, and with perfect conviction. My father thought the fire was an accident and the prosecuting witnesses perjured liars. I knew they were, because I held Major as friend. My father hired a lawyer to defend the obscure Negro.

In the end it was not the lawyer's art that brought Major off when the trial came on. Will Jones and his brother Calvin had come to town court-week on some infrequent errand. On the north side of the river little had been heard about the prisoner since his arrest, and they had been scarcely interested. But being in the courtroom when Major was arraigned they heard the fixing of dates during the preliminaries. It was noted that the fire occurred on the night preceding Thanksgiving Day. Will Jones turned to a stranger near by and remarked that Wiley Buck took him, his brother Calvin, and a neighbor named Thad Jacobs on their first possum hunt on that very night and that they had hunted all night. The stranger saw the importance of the evidence and immediately put Wiley Buck's lawyer and my father in touch with the Joneses. The result was swift acquittal.

Major, more ashen than ever, and wobbling from his long confinement, traveled home to his cabin. My father gave him a lift in our buggy. I sat between my father's knees and drove the gray mare. I was eager to hear Major talk, to express his relief from confinement. But the most he said was "Ah didn't done it," and "Ah wonners whar is ma dogs." We fed him in our kitchen when we reached home and he had stumblingly stalled the mare. We offered to make a pallet on the kitchen floor and keep him for the night. But he seemed restless, and the April night was mild. He said he would sleep by the river and cross over in the morning. Later I heard that Ed had been told by Calvin Jones of Major's coming, that the boy had met him at the river with one remaining cur.

At the cabin the antlers still hung crazily over the door. He rightened the trophy with a stone and some rusty nails. Now he was truly Wiley Buck again. Again he began to collect dogs and by winter was possessed of nine nondescript dependents. He ceased altogether to cross the river for work and partially attached himself to Will Jones for supplementary food in exchange for the bits of labor assigned him.

That winter was unusually rough for the region. Cold mists blew up from the coast. Snow lay on the ground for weeks on end. It made rabbit hunting easier for Wiley Buck; but the long cold nighttime, shut in the cabin with his dogs, was another matter. He had never taken thought for the morrow about coverings or fuel. Ed said he always slept with his dogs in winter. Certainly in that season, with no protection outside, the dogs were gathered into the cabin at night and the door well barred.

In late February, after a new fall of fluffy snow, Ed visited the cabin with a view to a possible rabbit hunt with his friend. As he approached the place he heard dismal howlings and whinings from the cabin. Nearer approach showed no tracks of man or dogs about the place. He called Wiley Buck. Response was the increased and excited howling of dogs on the inside. The boy was now scared. Here was something untoward. He found a stick and banged on the door. Only a louder clamor of the dogs. He tried the door with his shoulder without result.

Chance cast his glance toward the river, where he saw young Calvin Jones in a skiff with his gun. Calvin was out for ducks that sometimes made up the river in the late winter season.

The two youths beat open the door with difficulty—there was no window. Five weak and bloody dogs reeled out, their wolfish eyes burning with the light of thirst and famine. They gobbled up soft snow by the mouthful and glared at their rescuers. Calvin clutched his gun tight, and Ed held his stick. They spoke to the dogs soothingly, but the animals, despairing of food, moved wobblingly off toward water. Ed observed that these five were not all of Wiley Buck's dogs, though they were the largest and strongest. The overwhelming stench from the door now called the boys' attention back to the cabin and the possible fate of Wiley Buck. Peering into the half-gloom they saw the remains of stark tragedy. Naked bones and grisly skulls of dogs and a man littered the place. Tufts of dog hair intermingled with a few rags lay among the bones.

Within the hour the boys were at Will Jones's place with report of the horrible tale. Will journeyed back with them in a "carry-all," pulled by a raw-boned mule. They took a few tools, and gathered up a Negro man they passed.

After inspection at the cabin they scraped up the remains of man and dogs and buried them together in a hole they dug at the back of the cabin. Theory was, and doubtless fact, that Wiley Buck had suddenly died of a stroke, or perhaps heart failure. The dogs, shut in, and no one to hear their wailings, were finally driven to eat their master. Then they passed to killing each other, the smallest and weakest going first. Five of the nine had survived but these were gashed and torn when rescue came. One of these Calvin found dead next day by the river when he returned with Ed for his skiff. He had been partially eaten. The boys had brought some bread, out of pity for the dogs. This they scattered about the dead dog they found. Later Will Jones shot two others as they skulked about his place. They reminded him too vividly of the drama in the cabin. The remaining two were not seen again in that locality. They may have died at the water and floated away with the river.

Wiley Buck

As for Wiley Buck, I confess I wept all the way home from a crossroads store where Calvin Jones related the story to me in early spring. My father was also moved, though not as I—I, whose imagination the man had touched since I was eight years old. So I locked the story up in my mind, with no heart for the telling through all these years till now, now—after hardening to the sight of many other bits of God's flotsam cast about from one side of the River to another until they come to rest on a final shore.

"Old Man" John Bradsher—A Ghost Story

I was thirteen years old when I first saw a ghost. An old Negro man came to inform my father that a neighbor was dead, "old man" John Bradsher. Sometimes this man was called "Black Mouth John" to distinguish him from another John Bradsher who lived in the neighborhood. He wore a short and very bristly black beard over the whole of his face below the nose. He was an old bachelor, something of a recluse, and lived three miles up the river from our place. He had died alone in the night and was found next morning by a Negro woman who came to prepare his breakfast.

There was a strange story surviving in our neighborhood about this man, mainly kept alive among the Negroes. The gist of it was that when the Civil War came on and he rode off in the cavalry, he left behind on an adjoining farm a young woman with whom he was very much in love. When he returned after Appomattox she was dead and had been buried in her family burial place. After some months of quiet brooding, according to the story, the bereft ex-soldier, working at night, dug a grave in his own family burial place, exhumed the body of his beloved and reinterred her there. White people gave this tale little credence, regarding it largely as "Negro talk." Yet it could easily have been true, since both farms were quite isolated for lack of roads, and the young woman was the last of her line. Another interesting thing about Mr. Bradsher, and this was certainly true, he used the Rebel yell early every morning to roust out his Negro labor. And he was not unprosperous for the times.

"Old Man" John Bradsher—A Ghost Story

On the occasion of which I write, when Mr. Bradsher died, one of the Negroes on his place came for instructions to father, who was mentor and consultant to our whole community. The man was told to return, get other help, and prepare a grave in the family plot for the burial on the morrow. He, father, would attend to the further details when he drove into town that day.

Toward evening father returned tired. But he was concerned about whether the Negroes had faithfully carried out his directions about the grave. He decided to send me to see. I rode a fast horse and enjoyed the going, that is, until I had arrived at the Bradsher house. There as I approached the door on foot, I saw a white sheet over a body. The body was in the middle of the room on two planks whose ends were held up level by the seats of some chairs. Several Negro women were about in the room. One came to the door, greeted me, and asked if I would like to look at Mr. Bradsher "for the last time." I shrinkingly declined, with thanks for manners, and asked if the grave was finished. She thought it was, but suggested I go see for myself so as to be able to tell father for sure. I knew where the graveplot was, several hundred yards distant up through the undergrowth to a clump of trees. The path, rarely used, turned and twisted through the rather dense growth. At one nearly rightangle turn, I met "old man" Bradsher face to face right in the path. He stopped. I stopped. He never greeted me nor I him, though hitherto we had been friendly. I was greatly embarrassed and stepped quickly out of the path to be out of his way. I stumbled over a stone (it may have been a root) and when I righted myself Mr. Bradsher was gone.

Swiftly I decided neither to go back nor to go on. I circled an arc around to my horse. Then I rode! I rode like the wind! My horse was good and seemed to admit the importance of speed. Tam O'Shanter's mare, Meg, in her race from Kirk Alloway to the brig of Ayr, certainly would not have distanced me. I judge this from the fact that Tam's mare lost her tail in the pinch. Prince, my four-year-old roan, arrived with his. Even so it seemed a long way home.

There I reported to my father in terms he thought were incoherent and jumbled. But he was a good and tactful father. He said I was excited and sent me to bed. Next day he rode up, without me, and in the afternoon finished the obsequies of Black Mouth John. He said it went off all right, that there was a very respectable attendance for a weekday funeral.

www.ingramcontent.com/pod-product-compliance
Lightning Source LLC
Chambersburg PA
CBHW030117010526
44116CB00005B/287